Men's Fitness

MUSCLE
Food

MAGBOOK

Words Ben Ince
Art Director Rob Lavery
Recipes Karol Gladki,
Adam Gray, Alan Murchison
Photography
packshotfactory.co.uk
Additional photography
Thinkstock
Managing Editor Chris Miller
Men's Fitness Editor
Nick Hutchings

Group Publisher **Russell Blackman**
Group Managing Director **Ian Westwood**
International Business Development Director
Dharmesh Mistry
Digital Production Manager **Nicky Baker**
Operations Director **Robin Ryan**
Managing Director of Advertising
Julian Lloyd–Evans
Newstrade Director **David Barker**
Managing Director of Enterprise
Martin Belson
Chief Operating Officer/
Chief Financial Officer **Brett Reynolds**
Group Finance Director **Ian Leggett**
Chief Executive Officer **James Tye**
Chairman **Felix Dennis**

MUSCLE FOOD ISBN **1-78106-303-6**
To license this product please contact Nicole Adams on
+44 (0) 20 7907 6134 or nicole_adams@dennis.co.uk

Advertising
Simone Daws simone_daws@dennis.co.uk

REWRITE YOUR EXPECTATIONS

What do you expect from your pre-workout or mass gainer in terms of results? If you want more, if you want those around you to recognise those differences, then you have to optimise every part of your approach.

New Instant Mass Heavyweight delivers the following per 300g serving:

1,160	60g	3g	219g
calories	protein	Creapure® creatine	carbohydrate

Our newest and most calorie rich weight gainer formulated specifically for hard gainers and all athletes that demand a very high quality source of protein and complex carbohydrates. It is formulated to outperform in every area and will rewrite your expectations of what a weight gainer can deliver. Free from soy protein, corn syrup, fructose or other forms of sugar.

Just how serious are you about gaining mass?

New Muscle Bomb® pre-workout delivers the following per 30g serving;

7g	8g	3.2g	2.5g
BCAA	citrulline malate	beta-alanine	betaine anhydrous

2,000mg	1,000mg	250mg†
L-carnitine tartrate	L-taurine	caffeine

Categorically and factually one of the world's most, if not the most, potent pre-workout formula available delivering mega doses for all main ingredients in line with double blind scientific studies. Muscle Bomb® is also completely free from artificial colours and sweeteners. Caffeine-free version also available.

Do you know of another pre-workout product that delivers such dosages?

Perhaps the most important aspects of these products are their performance, mixability and taste which we believe are unbeaten

NATIVE WHEY
INSTANT MASS HEAVYWEIGHT
MUSCLE & STRENGTH

CHOW DOWN

Ben Ince, Editor

You can spend as many hours as you want in the gym – but if your nutrition isn't right you'll struggle to reach your muscle-building and fat-burning potential.

But fear not, healthy eating doesn't have to mean endless portions of chicken and broccoli. All the meals in this book will support your training and help you build the lean, ripped body you've always wanted, without breaking the bank or challenging your cooking skills. And every single one tastes delicious – which is kind of important!

We've arranged and categorised the recipes by their main ingredient - poultry, seafood, red meat, and eggs and dairy - and provided cooking time guidelines to ensure you'll always be able to find something tasty and convenient to meet your needs.

So grab your best chef's hat and apron, hit the kitchen and prepare to feast on some of the most appetising muscle-building you'll ever have tasted.

musclefood
Lean Meats Delivered To Your Door

'TRY US' BARGAIN BOX
USUALLY £64.89 - JUST £27

LIMITED STOCK AVAILABLE

23 ITEMS £1.17 PER ITEM

2 X 6-7oz Irish Grass Fed Rump Steaks
2 X 6-7oz Great British Hache Steaks
1 X 1.2kg-1.4kg Corn Fed Whole Chicken
4 X 4oz Great British Beef Steak Burgers
2 X 8-9oz Chicken Breast Fillets
1 X 227g Rosé Veal Escalope Steak
4 X 100g Pork Loin Steaks
6 X Pork Sausages (454g)
1 X Meat Seasoning

Super Chilled Delivery

Hydrated Ice Blocks →

Insulated Protective Wrap →

Insulated Inner Box →

Tough Exterior →

Also Includes
Free Recipe and Seasoning

SAVE £37.89

CONTENTS

NUTRITION
101

EATING DOESN'T NEED TO BE COMPLICATED, PROVIDED YOU FOLLOW THESE SIMPLE GUIDELINES

If you want to burn fat and build muscle, what you do in the kitchen is just as important as what you do in the gym. But knowing what advice to follow can be tricky. Every week sees new fad diets emerge, while nutritionists and scientists frequently contradict each other. To guide you through the confusion, we've distilled the wisdom of the world's leading nutrition experts into eight easy-to-follow guidelines. Keeping this advice in mind will help you understand the principles underpinning the meals in this book. So read on, digest and tuck in.

1 GREEN IS GOOD

There's no such thing as too much veg, especially if you're talking about vegetables grown above ground.

The Food Standards Agency's 'eatwell plate', the government-endorsed illustration of what to eat, suggests a third of your diet should come from fruit and veg. But it also suggests another third should be made up of 'bread, rice, potatoes and other starchy foods'. This is not the way to a lean body, because these simple carbohydrates cause rises in blood sugar, which leads to weight gain, type 2 diabetes and other health problems. Get your carbs from a more nutritious source with slower sugar release – which is almost every vegetable apart from potatoes.

It's also an oversimplification to put fruit and veg together. Eating a lot of fruit means eating excess fructose (fruit sugar), which also affects blood sugar. Veg doesn't contain fructose and is more nutrient-rich than fruit, so eat as many portions as you can.

THE SIMPLE VERSION Make vegetables the foundation of your diet and vary your veg intake as much as possible for the full range of nutrients.

2 EAT PROTEIN WITH EVERYTHING

You may meet someone at the gym or office who raises an eyebrow at the amount of protein you're ingesting. Some may even tell you confidently that it can be bad for your health. Here's the truth: the only studies that have ever suggested that protein can cause kidney problems were done on people with pre-existing kidney problems.

Protein is one of the most important components of the diet. Eating a high-protein diet means you feel fuller so you don't snack as muych – and lose weight as a result.

So what's the right amount? Estimates vary from 1-4g per kilo of bodyweight, per day, but most experts agree that 2g is the minimum. As for how much you can digest in one sitting, at least 20-25g is required for muscle-building levels of protein synthesis, and recent studies have found that the body can use nearly double that amount for building muscle.

What does this mean? For every meal, stick to a two-to-one ratio of vegetables to protein, by sight.

THE SIMPLE VERSION It's almost impossible to eat too much protein, although you could easily not be getting enough. Eat it with every meal.

3 DON'T BE AFRAID TO EAT FAT

Although most of us know that eating some fat is essential to a healthy diet, it's all too easy to make a mental connection between eating fat and getting fat, so you end up avoiding it.

It's true that at nine calories per gram, fat's more calorific than carbohydrate or protein, both of which only contain four. But if you're worried about your weight, the key is to eat foods that are genuinely satisfying, such as fat, because you'll eat less of them – and fewer snacks too.

Saturated fat has long been demonised as a cause of high cholesterol and heart disease. Recent research suggests, however, that in fact saturated fat raises 'good' HDL cholesterol levels while making 'bad' LDL cholesterol benign. Meanwhile the naturally-occurring fats found in oily fish, avocados, nuts, seeds, olives, olive oil and coconut oil provide you with essential fatty acids used for key functions such as metabolism and hormone synthesis, which are critical to your ability to burn fat.

The fats you should worry about are the man-made, hydrogenated variety found in processed foods and junk food. Research links them to a variety of illnesses and health issues, including heart disease and obesity.

THE SIMPLE VERSION Eat naturally occurring fats – including saturated fat – but avoid all processed, hydrogenated fats, especially trans fats.

4 STICK TO FREE RANGE

While bulk-buying cage-raised eggs might be tempting from a financial point of view, going for free-range – or even better organic – eggs, meat and fish is the far healthier choice.

Free-range chickens have a more varied diet and get more exercise than battery-farmed animals, so they develop more muscle. Their meat tends to contain more zinc, vitamins, amino acids and iron. Also, farm-raised salmon have been found to contain up to eight times the level of carcinogens of their wild brethren, thanks to cramped conditions and poor-quality feed, while grass-fed beef tends to have much higher levels of omega 3 fats than the kind fed on grain and beef tallow.

Eating free-range feels less like a luxury if you think of it this way: it's so nutritionally dissimilar to cage-reared that it's basically different food.

THE SIMPLE VERSION Eat free-range, grass-fed and wild-caught when you can. Don't know where it's from? Chances are the answer isn't good.

5 EAT REAL FOOD

This is the key. If you do this, you'll end up following all the other rules almost by default. A simple rule of thumb is only eat food that grows out of the ground or that once had a face.

Another option is to simply go caveman and think like a hunter-gatherer. When you're looking at something on the shelf, ask yourself if it would have existed 5,000 years ago. If the answer's no, it probably isn't anything you should be eating.

Another good healthy eating strategy is to stick to the outer aisles of the supermarket, which is where all the fresh produce is usually kept for ease of transportation, and away from the interior where everything's canned, processed or packed full of preservatives. Avoid food containing preservatives that you can't spell or ingredients you wouldn't keep in the kitchen. And eat things that will rot eventually, so you know they're fresh.

THE SIMPLE VERSION Eat food, rather than products pretending to be food.

6 DON'T COUNT CALORIES

Calories: the government is encouraging restaurants to put them on menus, women frantically add them up in the Tesco Express snack aisle, and people still treat the amount they burn off as the only thing that matters to fat loss.

That isn't the case, because calories are not a good indication of how healthy a food is and what effect it's going to have on your metabolic rate. Would you say a couple of poached eggs are the same as a can of Coke because they contain a similar number of calories?

Also, counting calories makes it easy to justify bad dietary decisions. Ever heard a friend say they can eat what they want because they'll burn it off at the gym? They couldn't be more wrong. In fact, the more active you are, the better your nutrition needs to be.

Arguably more important than calories is your food's glycaemic load (GL), which indicates how much of a blood sugar spike it'll give you – but manufacturers aren't required to put GL on packaging. But if you're following our rules this shouldn't be a problem. Steering clear of starchy food (such as pasta) and sugar means you're already avoiding foods with high GL.

You can also slow the absorption rate of high-GL foods, helping prevent blood sugar wobbles, by eating them with protein-heavy foods like chicken or tuna.

THE SIMPLE VERSION Think quality, not quantity. Eating nutritious food is better than sticking rigidly to a 2,000-calorie-a-day limit.

7 START AS YOU MEAN TO GO ON

Skipping breakfast won't necessarily have a negative impact on fat loss, as the standard advice used to say, but it's an ideal opportunity to take on nutrients that will sustain you through the day. However, you won't get the right things if you listen to the FSA's recommendation that you 'base your breakfast on bread or breakfast cereals,' and 'wash it down with some fruit juice'.

Eating a high-carb breakfast will give you low blood-sugar by mid-morning, making you more likely to snack on more high-carb foods, which creates a vicious circle of unhealthy snacking.

Instead of toast or cereal, have something low-carb that's more nutritionally sustainable, such as a plain full-fat yoghurt with berries and nuts or scrambled eggs with smoked salmon or ham. Avoid fruit juice too, because it's high in fructose but contains very little of the fibre found in whole fruit.

THE SIMPLE VERSION Think of breakfast like any other meal: you need a blend of protein, fats and fruit or veg.

8 LOSE THE BOOZE

It may sound obvious, but cutting back on your alcohol intake will have a huge impact on your attempts to lose weight and build muscle. Although rule 6 says calories aren't the be-all and end-all, the large quantities of nutritionally empty calories in alcohol won't improve your diet if you're looking to improve your body composition.

But the problems don't end there: alcohol stimulates your appetite when you're at your weakest – would you find a doner kebab appealing otherwise? What's more, the inevitable hangover will leave you feeling far less inclined to train the following day.

Which isn't to say that you shouldn't drink at all. A number of studies have found red wine offers tangible health benefits, thanks to its high polyphenol content that protects your heart from cardiovascular disease. But don't get too carried away – all the studies agreed that consuming more than two glasses a day would negate its positive effects.

THE SIMPLE VERSION Drink less booze. If you do drink, limit yourself to two small glasses of red wine per session.

Men's Fitness is no longer just a magazine – it's now available as an interactive issue on iPad, iPhone, Kindle Fire and Android and Windows devices. Each edition is full of expert advice on how to build muscle, shed body fat and improve your sporting performance, and now that comes alongside great interactive features including video content and the ability to save and store your favourite workouts.

Search for Men's Fitness UK magazine on your device and download the app today!

QUESTION TIME

No-nonsense answers to all your dietary queries,
courtesy of performance nutritionist Laurent Bannock

WHAT ARE THE HEALTHIEST CARBOHYDRATE SOURCES?

Grains such as wheat, oats and barley form the bulk of most people's carbohydrate intake in the standard Western diet. But eating these frequently – especially the processed kind – can lead to a variety of health problems, including weight gain. Luckily, fruit and vegetables also provide lots of carbs and eating them with every meal is enough provide your body with enough energy to fuel its daily activitiesand deliver crucial nutrients. Instead of grains, have a small amount of starchy veg such as yams and sweet potatoes with meals and snack on fruits such as apples and bananas, which contain healthy carbs.

WHICH OILS ARE THE BEST TO COOK WITH AND WHY?

The most important factor to consider when deciding which oil to use is its smoke point – the temperature at which it literally smokes, which is when it forms carcinogenic compounds such as HNE and free radicals. The smoke point of an oil is determined by how pure or refined it is – nothing to do with how much saturated fat it contains – because the refining process removes impurities from the oil, which generally raises the smoke point. So for high-heat cooking such as frying, grilling, stir-frying or roasting, use a light, refined oil such as olive oil, avocado oil, refined palm oil or coconut oil.

I'VE HEARD YOU SHOULDN'T EAT CARBS AT NIGHT. IS THAT TRUE?

You should try to avoid processed and refined carbohydrates at all times, because they offer little nutritional value. However, natural carb sources such as sweet potatoes, oats and vegetables provide a crucial fuel source for the body. These foods are best consumed after a workout, when their sugar content can actually help to improve muscle recovery and enhance hormonal adaptations. So if the evening is when you train, go ahead and eat plenty of healthy carbs afterwards – it will help you towards your fitness goals.

IS IT TRUE THAT I SHOULD AVOID FOODS LABELLED 'LOW FAT'?

Basically, yes. Most 'low-fat' foods have been highly processed to remove the fat and are also often packed with salt and sugar to enhance their flavour. It's also worth bearing in mind that natural fats found in foods such as oily fish, nuts, seeds, avocados, grass-fed beef, eggs and unprocessed dairy products are actually very good for you, and it's essential to obtain them from food since your body can't make them itself. The fats to avoid are the unhealthy, processed kind found in fried and junk foods.

ARE 'HEALTHY' BREAKFAST CEREALS REALLY HEALTHY?

The food industry often uses the term 'healthy' but it has no universally agreed meaning and can be misleading. Typically, a 'healthy' breakfast cereal is low in fat and has added vitamins. The problem is that it's often packed with sugar and has a lower nutrient density than its wholefood counterparts. Processing grains can lose more nutrients than are subsequently added, and fibre is usually low or nonexistent. Even 'high-fibre' cereals don't provide the best form of fibre for your gut and they can contain as many refined carbs as a cake. As a rule, 'healthy' breakfast cereals aren't healthy at all and don't support people's training or fat loss goals.

DAILY SERVINGS

Eat the right amount of the right foods to hit your training targets

VEGETABLES 8-10
These should form the main bulk of your carbohydrate intake, because they supply vital vitamins, minerals and disease-fighting phytochemicals. Most of these servings should be low-GL veg such as peppers, spinach and broccoli, although some can come from starchier sources such as sweet potatoes and beetroot.

MEAT, POULTRY, FISH AND EGGS 3-5
An active man needs extra protein for muscle repair and meat, poultry, fish and eggs

are the best natural sources. Protein is closely linked to fullness, so an increase in dietary protein should stop you from snacking too.

FRUIT 1-2
Fruits provide plenty of micronutrients, but they also tend to carry a heavy fructose load, which can spike insulin levels and lead to fat storage. For weight loss, choose low-fructose fruits such as melons and berries.

FATS AND OILS 2-3
Essential fats are so called because your body is unable to make them itself, while

healthy fats are crucial for vitamin absorption. Both can be found in avocado, olives, nuts and seeds.

DAIRY 1-2
While some dairy products are good sources of protein, they can contain excessive amounts of saturated fat as well as causing insulin spikes.

PROCESSED CARBS 1-2
For optimum nutrient intake you're far better off getting your carbs from vegetables. If you want a portion or two of simple carbs, go for porridge oats or wholegrain rice.

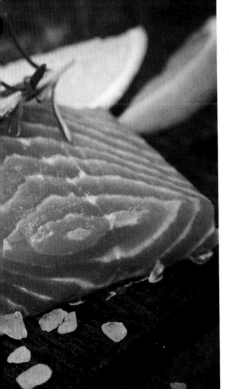

WHAT CAUSES HIGH CHOLESTEROL AND WHY IS IT BAD?

To talk of 'high cholesterol' is simplistic and unhelpful. Cholesterol is necessary to the body's functions. There are two types: high-density lipoprotein (HDL), known as 'good', which carries cholesterol away from arteries, and low-density lipoprotein (LDL), characterised as 'bad', which deposits it in artery walls, increasing your risk of heart disease. Generally, the cholesterol in food is poorly absorbed by the body, so eating high-cholesterol foods such as meat and dairy doesn't significantly increase levels. However, eating unsaturated fats (found in nuts and flaxseeds) has been shown to raise HDL and lower LDL levels.

WHICH WAY OF PRESERVING FOOD RETAINS THE MOST NUTRIENTS?

Freezing is particularly effective, especially when done at source. Canned food, such as tuna, is usually cooked first, which does reduce the nutrients, but the airtight can will then protect the contents from nutrient loss through oxidisation and airborne bacteria. Although drying reduces bacteria by removing water, it doesn't protect the food from oxidisation, which causes a loss of cell-protecting antioxidants. Food contains the most nutrients when it's fresh, but if you can't get fresh food, go for frozen, canned or dried, in that order.

WHAT SHOULD I DRINK AFTER MY WORKOUT?

Milk provides everything your body needs for recovery after training. One pint contains 30-35g protein, of which 20% is whey, which is absorbed quickly, while 80% is slow-release casein. Milk also contains glutamine and BCAAs to boost your immune system. Choose semi-skimmed milk, because fat slows absorption. If you're intolerant to cow's milk, try goat's. If you're trying to bulk up, have calorie-rich chocolate milk.

IS IT OK TO EAT WHOLEGRAIN CARBS IF I'M TRYING TO LOSE WEIGHT?

Brown rice, bread and pasta all contain fibre and are generally more nutritious than their white counterparts, but they're still high in carbohydrate. If you're overweight, you probably consume excess carbs already, so large quantities won't help, especially when you can get all the carbs and fibre your body needs by eating fruit and veg. If you can't live without brown carbs, eat them in small quantities to refuel after a fat-burning workout at the gym.

WILL EATING FRUIT MAKE ME FAT?

No – but drinking it will. Fruit is high in fructose, a form of sugar, but it's also high in fibre, which helps to control the body's response to sugar and neutralise its effect on insulin levels. In fruit juices and smoothies, most of – if not all – the fibre has been removed, causing the fructose to spike your insulin and encourage fat storage. Vegetables are a better source of fibre and contain little sugar – but a serving or two of fruit a day definitely won't make you fat.

HOW MUCH PROTEIN SHOULD I EAT IN ONE SITTING?

An average man – 1.78m and 78kg – should eat at least 20-25g of protein per feed to support muscle growth. If you have less than that, you'll struggle to get the recommended 2g per kilo of bodyweight in a day. You can eat more if you want to, though – it helps you feel full, and evidence shows the body can digest large amounts. Just remember no amount will help you build muscle mass if you're not exercising.

WHICH TYPES OF SUGAR ARE WORST FOR ME AND WHY?

Some forms of sugar are healthy, in small amounts, when found naturally within fruit and vegetables. However, when these sugars – such as fructose – are extracted they become far less healthy, because without the fibre and nutrients of the whole food they only add unnecessary 'empty' calories to your diet, often playing havoc with your blood sugar levels and causing weight gain. Refined, or processed, sugars such as sucrose are considered to play a key role in the global obesity pandemic, and are added to low-fat foods to make them taste better. You should try to avoid refined and processed sugars in all their forms, except when taken as part of a sports nutrition strategy.

HOW MUCH CAFFEINE SHOULD I DRINK AND WHEN?

Caffeine before training can stimulate your efforts in the gym and improve your ability to burn fat. However, if you have additional caffeine throughout the day its impact is reduced. Excess caffeine also raises your levels of the stress hormone cortisol, which can lead to fat storage and disrupted sleep. Limit your caffeine intake to one espresso 20 minutes before training. When you feel flat at other times, an apple can give you energy.

HOW MUCH FIBRE DO I NEED AND WHAT ARE THE BEST FOODS TO GET IT FROM?

Fibre helps food pass through your intestines, makes you feel full, stabilises blood sugar and boosts immunity. It's found in plant-based foods such as fruits, vegetables, grains and legumes. To get enough, aim to eat six to eight portions of vegetables and no more than one or two portions of wholegrains daily, while avoiding processed grains such as breakfast cereals because they've often had much of their fibre content removed as well as being low in nutrients and high in sugar.

Q SHOULD I CUT OUT GLUTEN?

A Despite the hype, most people aren't actually allergic or intolerant to gluten (a protein composite found in wheat). Symptoms of gluten intolerance include bloating and wind, but just because you feel bloated after eating bread, that doesn't necessarily mean you're reacting to gluten. Gliadin – the most problematic type of gluten – is commonly found in foods such as bread and pasta, but these cause separate digestion issues for most people anyway. The link between these symptoms and gluten is one of correlation rather than cause. Even if you are diagnosed with a reaction to gluten, you don't need to cut it out entirely – just scale back your consumption till you reach a point where the symptoms clear up. Provided you eat it in moderation, you should be fine.

Laurent Bannock is a sports scientist and performance nutritionist for pro rugby teams, and other elite athletes. For more visit guruperformance.com

NATURAL
WHEY
CO.

APPLE &
BLUEBERRY
SMOOTHIE
2.25KG

FITTER, HEALTHIER, STRONGER... THE NATURAL WHEY

PREMIUM QUALITY | naturally sweetened WITH REAL FRUIT | NO ADDED sugar | NO ARTIFICIAL FLAVOURINGS or COLOURINGS | TESTED and CERTIFIED

WWW.NATURALWHEYCOMPANY.COM | 🐦 @NATURALWHEYCO

RECIPE COURTESY OF THE FOOD MEDIC -
WWW.THEFOODMEDIC.WORDPRESS.COM

TRY THIS GREAT BRAMLEY APPLE & STRAWBERRY CRUMBLE RECIPE USING NATURAL WHEY CO PROTEIN
(SERVES 2-3)

INGREDIENTS:
1 LARGE APPLE
5 STRAWBERRIES
1 SCOOP OF THE NWC SMOOTHIE – BRAMLEY APPLE AND STRAWBERRY FLAVOUR
1/3 CUP (30G) OF OATS
1.5 TBSP OF AGAVE NECTAR OR HONEY
1.5 TBSP OF MELTED COCONUT OIL
CINNAMON

METHOD:
1. PREHEAT OVEN TO 180°
2. CHOP UP THE APPLE AND STRAWBERRIES AND PLACE IN A SMALL POT WITH ENOUGH WATER TO COVER THE BOTTOM. TURN ON THE HOB TO A LOW HEAT AND COVER THE POT, ALLOW SIMMER FOR 5-10 MINUTES TO SOFTEN THE FRUIT.
3. IN A BOWL COMBINE THE NWC SMOOTHIE, OATS AND CINNAMON.
4. NEXT ADD IN THE COCONUT OIL AND AGAVE NECTAR, STIRRING WELL TO ACHIEVE A CRUMBLEY TEXTURE – ADD MORE OIL IF IT FEELS TO DRY!
5. ADD THE FRUIT TO RAMEKINS, AND TOP WITH THE CRUMBLE MIXTURE.
6. BAKE IN THE OVEN FOR 10-15 MINUTES UNTIL GOLDEN BROWN – ALLOW COOL SLIGHTLY BEFORE EATING!

POULTRY

Chicken and **turkey** are both delicious and among the leanest and cheapest muscle-building protein sources around, while **duck** is rich in heart-healthy monounsaturated fats

UNDER
15
MINS

CHICKEN STIR-FRY

This speedy stir-fry recipe contains plenty of muscle-building veg and high-quality carbs to replenish your muscles after a tough workout

INGREDIENTS

Serves 1

250g chicken fillets

1 pack of egg noodles, cooked

1 pack of stir-fry vegetables

2 tbsp low-sodium soy sauce

1 tbsp sesame oil

1 tbsp sesame seeds

1 tbsp olive oil

TO MAKE

▷ Heat the olive oil in a frying pan or wok over a medium heat.

▷ Season the chicken and then add it to the pan, searing it for around two minutes on each side.

▷ Add the vegetables and noodles and fry for four minutes, stirring occasionally.

▷ Add the soy sauce, sesame oil and seeds, stir through to warm and serve immediately.

THE BENEFITS

CHICKEN
is an excellent source of protein and vitamin B3, which helps to prevent your body from storing fat

EGG NOODLES
contain protein to build muscle and carbs to replenish your glycogen stores and give you energy.

SESAME SEEDS
contain selenium, which kills off harmful free radicals that interfere with muscle growth

CHICKEN CHILLI SALAD

This spicy salad is quick, easy to prepare and rich in muscle-building protein and metabolism-boosting capsaicin

INGREDIENTS

Serves 1

1 chicken breast

1tbsp ginger, grated

2tbsp olive oil

½ a mango, sliced

A handful of spinach

A small handful of coriander leaves

½ a chilli, diced

Juice of **½** a lemon

TO MAKE

- Marinate the chicken breast with the ginger and half the olive oil for ten minutes.
- Grill the chicken breast for ten to 12 minutes, turning halfway through cooking, then remove and cut into strips.
- Mix the strips with the mango, spinach, coriander and chilli in a bowl.
- Dress with lemon juice and the rest of the olive oil.

THE BENEFITS

CHILLI
is full of capsaicin, which can fight inflammation and soothe your aching muscles after a workout

SPINACH
is rich in folate, which encourages your body to convert proteins and sugars into energy

MANGO
contains fibre, pectin and vitamin C to help lower LDL ('bad') cholesterol levels in the blood

UNDER
15
MINS

CHICKEN KEBABS

Ditch that unhealthy takeaway and feast at home with this cheap and tasty kebab recipe, packed with muscle-building protein

INGREDIENTS

Serves 1

1 chicken breast, cubed

4 mushrooms, halved

4 medium tomatoes, halved

1 red pepper, cut into segments

1 onion, cut into six pieces

1 large wholemeal pitta bread

2tbsp Greek yogurt

A handful of iceberg lettuce, shredded

TO MAKE

▷ Place the chicken and vegetable pieces on a skewer.

▷ Grill the skewer for ten minutes, turning frequently.

▷ Toast the pitta for one to two minutes each side.

▷ Serve the chicken and vegetables with the pitta, Greek yogurt and lettuce.

CHICKEN
helps to improve your ratio of good to bad cholesterol by providing vitamin B3

MUSHROOMS
are packed with fibre to keep you feeling full and help you resist the urge to snack

GREEK YOGURT
contains protein as well as pantothenic acid, a vitamin that helps convert food into fuel

UNDER
15
MINS

CHICKEN WITH VEG

This summer veg-based dish is a simple, delicious muscle-building meal that tastes great and takes just minutes to make

INGREDIENTS

Serves 1

1 organic chicken breast

1 red pepper, chopped

50g cherry tomatoes, halved

A handful of spinach, chopped

50g green beans, trimmed and halved

A handful of pitted black olives

2tbsp olive oil

1tbsp balsamic vinegar

1tbsp capers

TO MAKE

- Preheat the grill to 180°C.

- Butterfly the chicken breast and season it with a little salt and pepper and half the olive oil, then grill it for eight minutes, turning halfway through.

- Meanwhile, heat the rest of the olive oil in a pan on a medium heat, then add the green beans, peppers and capers to the pan and cook for four minutes, stirring occasionally.

- Add the tomatoes and olives and cook for a further two minutes.

- Add the spinach and seasoning and cook for a further minute.

- Place the veg mix on a plate with the chicken on top and garnish it with the balsamic vinegar.

THE BENEFITS

CHICKEN
offers lots of muscle-building protein and very little fat

SPINACH
is full of iron, which supplies muscles with oxygen to help you exercise

TOMATOES
contains plenty of vitamin C, which helps your body form strong tendons, ligaments and bone tissue

CHICKEN OMELETTE

Omelettes are a great option if you want to feast on protein without spending a fortune or endless hours in the kitchen

INGREDIENTS

Serves 1

50g chicken, sliced

5 cherry tomatoes, chopped

4 mushrooms, chopped

3 fresh eggs

10g cheddar cheese, grated

1tbsp of butter

30g spinach

Black pepper, to season

TO MAKE

- Fry the chicken in a pan for five to seven minutes, then remove.
- Cook the tomatoes and mushrooms in the pan for two minutes, then remove.
- Whisk the eggs and cook for five minutes.
- Turn the eggs onto a plate and add the cheese and other toppings.
- Garnish with the spinach.

THE BENEFITS

EGG
contains all the essential amino acids, making it a complete protein source that keeps you feeling full

SPINACH
is packed with vitamin K, which strengthens bones

CHEDDAR
offers CLA, a naturally occurring fatty acid proven to help build muscle and reduce body fat

UNDER
15
MINS

CHICKEN FAJITA

This classic Tex-Mex dish provides plenty of muscle-building protein, plus a chilli kick that will ramp up your metabolism and burn more calories

INGREDIENTS

Serves 2

2 skinless chicken breasts, cut into strips

1tbsp olive oil

1tsp chilli flakes

1 onion, diced

1 red pepper, cut into slices

200g chopped tomatoes

A handful of coriander

4 wholemeal tortillas

2tbsp Greek yogurt

1 avocado, cubed

TO MAKE

▷ Heat the oil in a wok until it begins to smoke.

▷ Add the chicken strips and fry them for four minutes.

▷ Add the onions and peppers and fry for a further three minutes.

▷ Add the chilli flakes and the chopped tomatoes and fry for another three minutes.

▷ Warm the wraps for two minutes under a pre-heated grill.

▷ Spoon the mixture into the wraps and dress them with the coriander, yogurt and avocado.

THE BENEFITS

ONIONS
are packed with quercetin, an antioxidant with potent anti-inflammatory properties

GREEK YOGURT
provides probiotics that promote intestinal health

AVOCADO
offers unsaturated fats, which help to lower body fat and reduce blood pressure

UNDER
60
MINS

CHICKEN TAGINE

With or without a tagine pot, this Moroccan classic makes for a delicious, protein-packed muscle-building treat

INGREDIENTS

Serves 3-4

8 small chicken thighs

3tbsp olive oil

2 medium onions, chopped

2 garlic cloves, crushed

A large pinch of saffron threads, crushed

1tsp ground ginger

1tsp ground cumin

1tsp ground cinnamon

400g canned chopped tomatoes

10 dried apricots, quartered

1 lemon, juiced

2tbsp honey

A small handful of chopped coriander

300ml chicken stock

4tbsp flaked almonds, toasted

200g couscous

TO MAKE

- Heat the oil in a tagine pot if you have one – if not, a large, heavy-bottomed saucepan is fine.

- Season the chicken with salt and pepper. Add to the pan and brown on both sides. Remove and set to one side.

- Add the remaining oil, onions and garlic to the pan and sauté for ten minutes. Add the spices and stir in for one minute.

- Stir in the tomatoes, chicken, apricots, lemon juice, honey and half the coriander. Pour in the stock and cook over a low heat for 30 minutes until the chicken is tender.

- Sprinkle the almonds and the remaining coriander over the top and serve.

THE BENEFITS

CHICKEN
has a whopping 10g of protein in each thigh to help you build muscle

ONION
offers high levels of chromium, which prevents insulin spikes so you don't store fat

CUMIN
contains capsaicin, which ramps up your metabolism for more efficient fat-burning

CHICKEN TANDOORI

Got time to make a show-stopping curry? As well as tasting delicious, this one will fire up your metabolism to burn more fat

INGREDIENTS

Serves 2

6 skinless, boneless chicken thighs

1 red onion, finely chopped

1 lemon, juiced

2tsp paprika

1tbsp olive oil

100g brown rice, cooked

FOR THE MARINADE

150ml Greek yogurt

1tbsp grated ginger

2 garlic cloves, crushed

½tsp garam masala

½tsp ground cumin

½tsp chilli powder

½tsp turmeric

TO MAKE

▷ Mix all the marinade ingredients together in a bowl, add the chicken thighs and leave to marinate for 60-90 minutes.

▷ In a separate bowl, mix the onion with the lemon juice and paprika.

▷ Grill the chicken under a medium heat for eight minutes on each side, ensuring it's thoroughly cooked.

▷ Grill the onions for two to three minutes.

▷ Mix the onions with the brown rice and serve with the chicken.

THE BENEFITS

CHICKEN
provides high levels of B vitamins, which boost energy

RED ONION
is higher in polyphenols – including soothing quercetin – than other onion varieties

GREEK YOGURT
is an excellent source of joint-soothing omega 3

UNDER **60** MINS

CHICKEN KORMA

Don't scoff a criminally greasy takeaway – get good fats and protein with this healthy home-made curry recipe

INGREDIENTS

Serves 2

3 skinless chicken breasts, diced

100ml rapeseed oil

1 red onion, finely chopped

1 cinnamon stick, halved

2 red chillies, deseeded and finely chopped

2 garlic cloves, crushed

8 green cardamom pods

3 cloves

50g fresh ginger, finely chopped

2 fresh or dried bay leaves

Salt and black pepper to taste

300ml natural Greek yogurt

200ml chicken stock

40g cashew nuts

A handful of fresh coriander, chopped

200g brown rice

TO MAKE

◗ Heat half the rapeseed oil in a pan over a medium heat.

◗ Add the red onion, cinnamon, chilli and garlic and cook for five to eight minutes, stirring occasionally.

◗ Add the cardamom, cloves, ginger and bay leaves and cook on a low heat for ten to 12 minutes.

◗ Meanwhile, heat the remaining rapeseed oil in a separate pan over a high heat.

◗ Season the chicken, add to the second pan and cook until golden brown on all sides.

◗ Remove and drain in a colander to remove any excess oil. Add to the onion and spices in the other pan and mix thoroughly.

◗ Cover with the yogurt, cashew nuts and stock, and simmer gently for 20–25 minutes.

◗ Once the chicken is fully cooked, add the coriander and mix.

◗ Serve with the brown rice, cooked according to packet instructions.

THE BENEFITS

CASHEW NUTS
provide high levels of heart–healthy monounsaturated and polyunsaturated fats

RED ONIONS
are one of the best dietary sources of biotin, which helps control blood sugar, aiding fat loss

CHICKEN
is high in selenium, which protects against cell damage caused by intense exercise

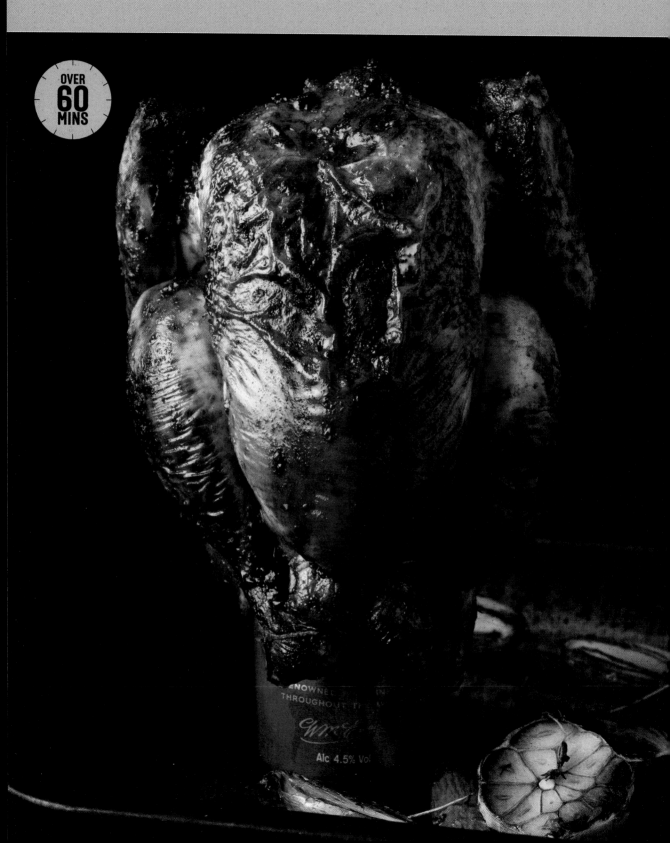

OVER
60
MINS

RENOWNED
THROUGHOUT THE

Gwr

Alc 4.5% Vol

BEER CAN CHICKEN

When it comes to building muscle, beer is your sworn enemy – unless you're marinating your chicken in it

INGREDIENTS

Serves 4-6

1 large free range chicken

2tbsp olive oil

2 onions, diced

4 cloves of garlic, chopped

2tbsp tomato purée

100g raisins

100g prunes

100ml white wine vinegar

200ml orange juice

50ml lemon juice

150g sugar

440ml can of beer

A pinch of chilli powder

A pinch of cayenne pepper

A pinch of smoked paprika

TO MAKE

- Fry the onion and garlic in the oil until soft. Add the purée, raisins and prunes and cook for two to three minutes. Add the vinegar, juice, sugar and 300ml of beer and simmer for five to six minutes.

- Blend in a food processor until smooth and add the spices. Marinade the chicken in this mixture in the fridge for at least two hours.

- Preheat the oven to 200°C/gas mark 6.

- Insert the can (containing the remaining 140ml of beer) open end first into the chicken's rear end. Stand up on the can in a roasting tray and cook for 50-60 minutes until piping hot, basting occasionally.

- Allow to stand for 10-15 minutes. Serve with brown rice and green vegetables.

THE BENEFITS

OLIVE OIL
is high in heart-healthy unsaturated fats

CHILLI POWDER
is rich in capsaicin, which boosts your metabolism, burning more fat

PRUNES
are packed with fibre that's essential for good gut health

CHICKEN & SPINACH PIZZA

Create a fat-burning feast by swapping the blood sugar-spiking doughy disc for an alternative made of cauliflower and chickpeas

INGREDIENTS

Serves 2

FOR THE BASE

120g chickpea flour

200g raw cauliflower, grated

½tsp baking powder

1tsp ground cumin

1tsp ground coriander

3 spring onions, finely chopped

160ml semi-skimmed milk

50ml rapeseed oil

Salt and pepper

FOR THE TOPPING

200g cooked free-range chicken breast, sliced

300g passata

50g baby spinach leaves

50g Parmesan cheese, grated

TO MAKE

○ Mix the chickpea flour, cauliflower, baking powder, cumin, coriander and spring onions together in a bowl.

○ Slowly add the milk and mix until it forms a dough. Season to taste.

○ Cover the bowl with cling film and place in the fridge for ten minutes.

○ Place the dough on a clean work surface. Gently press flat until you have a disc the size of a small dinner plate about 5mm thick.

○ Place the pizza base on a baking tray that has been lightly greased with half the rapeseed oil.

○ Spread the passata evenly over the base, then arrange the chicken and spinach on top. Pour the remaining rapeseed oil on top and finish with a layer of grated Parmesan.

○ Bake in the oven at 180°C/gas mark 4 for 18-20 minutes, or until the base is golden brown and the topping has melted.

THE BENEFITS

SPINACH
is rich in energy-
boosting folate

CORIANDER
contains high levels of
manganese, which helps
the body to metabolise fat

CAULIFLOWER
is an excellent source
of immunity-boosting
vitamin C

OVER
60
MINS

COQ AU VIN

Women love a good cook, right? Impress on date night with this seductive chicken dish that'll also give you a hit of muscle-building protein

INGREDIENTS

Serves 2

4 chicken legs, skinned

½ a bottle of red wine

1 tbsp olive oil

100g button mushrooms

100g carrots, peeled and chopped

100g shallots, peeled

50g smoked back bacon, sliced

A pinch of thyme

1 bay leaf

1 litre chicken stock

A pinch of chopped parsley

10g cornflour, mixed into a paste with cold water

TO MAKE

▷ Mix the chicken, mushrooms, shallots, carrots, thyme and bay leaf with the red wine and leave to marinate for two hours.

▷ Remove the chicken and fry it lightly in a pan with the olive oil.

▷ Place the chicken in a deep casserole dish with the vegetables, wine and chicken stock and bake it in an oven pre-heated to 180°C/gas mark 4 for two hours.

▷ Drain the liquid into a saucepan and stir in the cornflour paste to thicken it.

▷ Serve the chicken, then cover it with the sauce and the parsley.

▷ Enjoy with a large glass of red wine.

THE BENEFITS

MUSHROOMS
contain high levels of zinc, which helps fight off infection

ONIONS
are packed with potassium, which is essential for a healthy cardiovascular system

RED WINE
can contribute to fat loss and heart health with its high levels of resveratrol – when drunk in moderation

COBB SALAD

Who said salad can't be manly? The mighty Cobb contains eggs, chicken and bacon to provide a massive serving of protein

INGREDIENTS

Serves 1

1 chicken breast

3 rashers of bacon

1 hard-boiled egg

A handful of cherry tomatoes, halved

30g blue cheese, crumbled

A handful of iceberg lettuce, sliced

A handful of Romaine lettuce, sliced

A handful of watercress, sliced

1tbsp chives, chopped

Salt and black pepper to taste

FOR THE DRESSING
2tbsp olive oil

1tbsp red wine vinegar

1tbsp fresh lemon juice

½tbsp dry mustard

½tsp Worcestershire sauce

1 garlic clove, crushed

Salt and black pepper to taste

TO MAKE

- Grill the chicken breast for four minutes on each side under a medium heat.
- Grill the bacon alongside the chicken for three minutes on each side.
- Add a pinch of salt to a pan of boiling water and boil your egg for eight minutes.
- Meanwhile, mix the cheese, tomato, lettuce, watercress and chives.
- In a separate bowl, mix the dressing ingredients, then add the dressing to the salad bowl and mix well.
- Peel and slice the egg and slice the chicken.
- Top the salad with the chicken, bacon and egg.

THE BENEFITS

CHICKEN
fights infections by providing selenium

TOMATO
contains immunity-boosting vitamin C as well as biotin, which helps metabolise fat

BLUE CHEESE
is high in muscle-building protein and calcium to strengthen your bones

UNDER
15
MINS

CLUB SANDWICH

This fitness-focused upgrade of the classic club features waistline-friendly onion jam instead of the blubber-inducing mayonnaise

INGREDIENTS

Serves 1

½ a chicken breast, grilled and sliced

2 rashers of smoked back bacon

½ an avocado

1 tomato

Handful of spinach

1tbsp onion jam

3 thin slices of wholemeal toast

TO MAKE

- Grill the sliced chicken breast for four minutes each side under a medium heat and grill the bacon for three minutes on each side.

- Cut the tomato and avocado into four thick slices each.

- Toast the bread and spread half the onion jam on the first layer.

- Add a layer of chicken and bacon, then a second layer of toast. Spread it with the remaining onion jam.

- Add a layer of avocado, tomato and spinach followed by the final layer of toast. Press it, slice it and serve.

THE BENEFITS

BACON
contains 12g of muscle-building protein per 100g, as well as testosterone-boosting zinc

AVOCADO
is high in heart-healthy fats and a variety of anti-inflammatory antioxidants

WHOLEMEAL BREAD
provides filling fibre and energy-sustaining slow-release carbs

CHICKEN WINGS

Skip the buffet queue and feast on grease-free chicken wings at home with this sweet and spicy recipe

INGREDIENTS

Serves 2-4

12 free-range or organic chicken wings

100ml rapeseed oil

1tbsp pure maple syrup

1tsp English mustard

½tsp cayenne pepper

1tbsp hot smoked paprika

70ml red wine vinegar

Salt and pepper to taste

TO MAKE

▷ Mix all the ingredients except the chicken in a bowl with a spatula until they form a paste.

▷ Coat the chicken wings thoroughly with the marinade.

▷ Place the wings on a roasting tray in an oven pre-heated to 180°C/gas mark 4 for 20 minutes.

▷ Serve with fresh lime slices and roasted sweet potato wedges.

THE BENEFITS

PAPRIKA
contains metabolism-boosting capsaicin

ENGLISH MUSTARD
contains selenium, which soothes muscle inflammation

MAPLE SYRUP
is lower in sugars than alternatives such as honey, and also provides bone-building manganese

ROAST DUCK

This protein-packed bird makes a delicious roast – if you follow this foolproof guide

INGREDIENTS

Serves 4

1 duck

3 oranges

A handful of fresh thyme

5 cloves of garlic

2tbsp olive oil

TO MAKE

▷ Preheat the oven to 180°C/gas mark 4.

▷ Remove the giblets from inside the duck and trim the fat from the outside.

▷ Stuff the duck with half an orange and all the thyme and garlic. Halve the remaining oranges and place them in a large roasting tray with the duck and the olive oil.

▷ Cook, basting occasionally, for around 1½ hours or until the juices run clear.

▷ When the duck is fully cooked, let it sit for ten minutes before serving.

THE BENEFITS

DUCK
is a great source
of heart-healthy
monounsaturated fats

ORANGES
are rich in immunity-
boosting vitamin C

GARLIC
contains muscle-soothing
anti-inflammatory
compounds

ROAST TURKEY

Sick of Sunday evening bloat?
Reinvent your roast by adding these
unconventional fat-burning side dishes

INGREDIENTS

Serves 4-6

2-2.5kg turkey breast, boned and rolled

100ml rapeseed oil

8 medium sweet potatoes, peeled and evenly chopped

2 bunches of Chantenay or baby carrots, washed

½ a bunch of fresh tarragon leaves, roughly chopped

1tbsp natural yogurt

1 medium cauliflower, cut into 3cm pieces

½ a loaf of wholemeal bread

2tbsp dried cranberries, roughly chopped

2tbsp dried sage

2tbsp mature cheddar, grated

500g baby spinach, washed

Salt and pepper

TO MAKE

Roast turkey
- Heat the oven to 220°C/gas mark 7.

- Cover the turkey with half the oil, and season. Roast for 20 minutes, then reduce the heat to 170°C/gas mark 3 and cook for another 50 minutes, or until the juices run clear.

- Remove from the oven and leave to rest. When the meal is ready to serve, return to the oven at 170°C for ten minutes. Use the juices for gravy.

Roast sweet potatoes
- Heat the oven to 220°C/gas mark 7.

- Place the sweet potato in a pan of cold water. Bring to the boil, simmer for one minute, then drain.

- Pour the remaining oil into a warmed roasting tray, then add the sweet potato.

- Roast for 30 minutes, turning the potatoes halfway through. Season before serving.

Cauliflower with toasted cranberry breadcrumbs
- Bring a pan of water to the boil. Add the cauliflower and simmer for four minutes.

- Blend the bread in a food processor. Mix the breadcrumbs in a bowl with the cranberries, sage and cheese.

- Place the drained cauliflower in a heatproof dish. Sprinkle with the breadcrumb mix and brown under a medium grill.

Baby carrots with tarragon
- Bring a pan of water to the boil and add the carrots. Simmer for three to four minutes, then drain.

- Return the carrots to the pan and add the tarragon and yogurt. Mix thoroughly.

THE BENEFITS

CHEDDAR CHEESE
is a great source of energy-boosting vitamin B12

SWEET POTATOES
have a low GL and help to regulate blood sugar levels

TURKEY
is a lean source of muscle-building protein

UNDER
30
MINS

TURKEY CURRY

This spicy recipe will help fire up your metabolism to burn more calories

INGREDIENTS

Serves 2

250g cold roast turkey breast, cut into chunks

1tsp olive oil

1 onion, diced

2 garlic cloves, crushed

3 green chillies, diced

1 green pepper, sliced

2cm fresh ginger, grated

1tsp ground cumin

1tsp ground coriander

1tsp turmeric

½tsp garam masala

1tsp tomato purée

400g can chopped tomatoes

1tsp lemon juice

60ml water

A handful of fresh coriander, chopped

Salt and pepper, to season

TO MAKE

▷ Heat the oil in a pan. Add the onion, garlic, chillies, pepper and ginger, and cook over a high heat.

▷ After two minutes, lower the heat and add all the spices.

▷ After a further two minutes, add the tomato purée, chopped tomatoes, lemon juice and water. Stir and simmer for ten minutes.

▷ Place the mixture in a blender and blend until you have a smooth sauce. Return the sauce to the pan, add the turkey and cook gently until the turkey is warmed through.

▷ Add the coriander and serve.

THE BENEFITS

CHILLIES
contain vitamin E, which helps reduce your LDL ('bad') cholesterol levels

GREEN PEPPER
provides plenty of immunity-boosting vitamins A and C

TURKEY
is rich in energy-boosting vitamin B3

GREEN THAI CURRY

This Thai classic gives you a hit of lean protein and contains metabolism-boosting spices to help burn fat and reveal your muscles

INGREDIENTS

Serves 2

300g chicken fillets, diced

100g fresh ginger, grated

2 sticks of lemongrass, finely chopped

1 fresh chilli, finely chopped

1tbsp olive oil

2tbsp Thai green curry paste

1 can of coconut milk

450ml water

1 chicken stock cube

1 pack of straight-to-wok fine noodles

1 bag of mixed stir-fry veg

2tbsp Thai fish sauce

Juice of one lime

A bunch of fresh coriander, finely chopped

TO MAKE

▷ Pre-heat a large non-stick saucepan.

▷ Add the ginger, lemon grass, chilli and olive oil and cook over a medium heat for three to four minutes.

▷ Add the coconut milk, water and stock cube, bring to the boil and simmer for seven to eight minutes.

▷ Add the chicken and simmer for five minutes.

▷ Add the vegetables and noodles, then remove from the heat.

▷ Set aside for five minutes and then season with the fish sauce, lime juice and coriander.

THE BENEFITS

COCONUT MILK
is rich in heart-healthy fats

CHILLIES
are a source of iron, which carries oxygen through the bloodstream, helping you train hard

LIME JUICE
blunts insulin response to help avoid fat storage

CRISPY DUCK

If you only ever eat duck from your local Chinese takeaway, it's time to sharpen your knives and go it alone

INGREDIENTS

Serves 3-4

1 duck, backbone removed

1 small red cabbage

2 carrots

1 red onion

6tbsp natural yogurt

4 handfuls of watercress, washed and drained

100ml freshly squeezed orange juice

1 orange

1tbsp clear honey

150ml rapeseed oil

Salt and pepper to taste

TO MAKE

Crispy duck

▷ Preheat your oven to 210°C/gas mark 6-7.

▷ Flatten the duck by pressing it down firmly on a chopping board, then place it skin-side up on a rack over a roasting tray and pierce the skin all over with a sharp knife or metal skewer.

▷ Boil a kettle and pour the boiling water over the duck skin. Pat dry with kitchen roll and rub salt and pepper over the skin to taste.

▷ Place the duck in the oven and roast for an hour or until it's crisp and golden brown. Remove and let it rest for ten minutes.

▷ Remove all the skin and meat from the carcass and shred it using two forks. Place it on kitchen roll to remove any excess oil.

Red cabbage coleslaw

▷ Remove the white core from the red cabbage and finely chop it. Peel the carrots and grate them. Peel the red onion, cut it in half and finely slice it.

▷ Mix the cabbage, carrot and onion with the natural yogurt. Season with salt and pepper to taste.

Honey and orange sauce

▷ Place the orange juice in a saucepan. Bring it to the boil, then whisk in the honey.

▷ Remove from the heat and whisk in the oil.

To serve

▷ Return the shredded crispy duck to the oven for five minutes to heat through.

▷ Spoon coleslaw onto a place and scatter the watercress and orange segments around it. Place crispy duck on the coleslaw and drizzle orange honey sauce over the meat.

THE BENEFITS

DUCK
is packed with muscle-building protein

NATURAL YOGURT
is one of the richest sources of vitamin B2, which provides energy

ORANGE
is rich in immunity-strengthening vitamin A

CHICKEN & MUSHROOM RISOTTO

Our fitness-boosting take on risotto is satisfying, quick to make and fuels your workouts

INGREDIENTS

Serves 3-4

4 chicken breasts, diced

25g unsalted butter

1 small onion, finely chopped

2 cloves of garlic, crushed

250g button mushrooms, sliced

350g orzo pasta

400ml chicken stock

250g chestnut or shiitake mushrooms, finely sliced

2tbsp olive oil

2tbsp crème fraîche

3tbsp fresh parmesan, grated

1 small bunch of fresh tarragon, finely chopped

TO MAKE

▷ Heat half the olive oil in a pan over a medium heat and add the diced chicken breast. Sauté for four to five minutes, then set to one side.

▷ In a separate pan, gently cook the onion and garlic in the butter for three to four minutes over a medium heat until soft, then add the mushrooms and cook for a further five minutes.

▷ In another pan, simmer the orzo in 300ml of water with the stock over a medium heat for nine minutes until soft, then drain.

▷ Mix the orzo and the chicken with the mushroom mixture and heat gently over a low heat for three to four minutes.

▷ Stir in the crème fraîche, parmesan and tarragon, then remove from the heat and serve.

THE BENEFITS

MUSHROOMS
are rich in filling fibre

ONIONS
contain copper, which helps keep bones healthy by manufacturing collagen in the body

PARMESAN
is a source of bone-strengthening calcium

CHICKEN WALDORF SALAD

This update on the venerable New York salad adds protein-rich chicken to build and repair lean muscle, as well as a fat-burning dressing

INGREDIENTS

Serves 1

½ a red apple, chopped

½ a stalk of celery, peeled and chopped

100g cooked chicken, chopped

15g walnuts

½ a head of baby gem lettuce, chopped

1tsp parsley, chopped

2tbsp natural yogurt

1tsp Dijon mustard

1tbsp lemon juice

TO MAKE

▷ Mix the apple, celery, chicken, walnuts, lettuce and parsley in a bowl.

▷ In a separate bowl, make the dressing by mixing the yogurt, mustard and lemon juice with a whisk.

▷ Serve the salad and garnish it with the dressing.

▷ Season with salt and pepper to taste.

THE BENEFITS

WALNUTS
are a source of joint-soothing omega 3 fatty acids

NATURAL YOGURT
is rich in energy-boosting vitamin B12

APPLES
contain polyphenols that help reduce fat-storing blood sugar spikes

SEAFOOD

Eating for muscle isn't just about meat –
mix things up with these delicious seafood
recipes, including omega 3-rich **salmon** and
tuna, a great-value source of protein

PRAWN STIR-FRY

Enjoy protein-packed shellfish with fresh vegetables in minutes with this quick and easy stir-fry recipe

INGREDIENTS

Serves 1

1tbsp olive oil

100g of raw prawns, peeled

100g of Queen scallops

2 pak choi, cut into quarters

1 chilli, chopped

1tbsp chopped ginger

A handful of chopped coriander leaves

1tbsp low-sodium soy sauce (optional)

Juice of 1 lemon (optional)

TO MAKE

▷ Heat the olive oil in a wok on a high heat.

▷ Add the prawns and scallops to the wok and cook for three minutes, stirring occasionally.

▷ Add the pak choi, chilli, ginger and coriander and cook for a further three minutes.

▷ Serve, garnishing with your choice of soy sauce, lemon juice or just a little salt and black pepper.

THE BENEFITS

GINGER
has anti-inflammatory properties and has been shown to aid digestion

CHILLIES
are a source of capsaicin, which ups your metabolic rate, causing your body to burn more calories

PRAWNS
contain plenty of protein and vitamin B12 to help you pack on muscle

PAELLA

Carb up and repair your muscles after a tough workout with this tasty Spanish recipe

INGREDIENTS

Serves 4–6

12 prawns

12 mussels

2 chicken breasts, chopped

4–6 chicken wings

200g chorizo, chopped

1tbsp olive oil

2 cloves garlic, crushed

1 red pepper, sliced

½tsp smoked paprika

300g paella rice

1litre chicken stock

8 cherry tomatoes, halved

A pinch of saffron

400g can cannellini beans

50g frozen peas

TO MAKE

- Warm the oil in a frying pan or wok over a medium heat.

- Add the chicken and fry, turning occasionally, until it's slightly browned on all sides.

- Add the garlic, peppers, paprika and rice and fry for two to three minutes.

- Add the chorizo, stock, cherry tomatoes and saffron and cook for ten minutes.

- Add the cannellini beans and peas and cook for another ten minutes.

- Add the seafood and cook for a further ten minutes. If the liquid fully reduces, top up with boiling water to ensure the paella doesn't dry out and stick.

THE BENEFITS

CANNELLINI BEANS
are an excellent source of fibre to fill you up and reduce snacking

PRAWNS
are high in selenium, which protects your body's cells from the stress of exercise

RICE
is full of carbs to help you recover after your evening workout

UNDER
15
MINS

SALMON FILLET

From fridge to plate in minutes – enjoy this easy, healthy fish dish with a hefty serving of nutritious green veggies

INGREDIENTS

Serves 1

200g salmon fillet

1 pack of asparagus tips

100g peas

A handful of spinach

2tbsp extra virgin olive oil

1 lemon

TO MAKE

◊ Preheat the grill to 180°C/gas mark 4.

◊ Place the salmon on a baking tray and grill it for eight minutes, turning halfway through.

◊ Meanwhile, warm a pan over a medium heat and add half the olive oil.

◊ Add the asparagus tips to the pan and fry for three minutes until tender, stirring occasionally.

◊ Add the peas and cook for another two minutes.

◊ Add the spinach and cook for a further two minutes.

◊ Serve the salmon with the vegetables and dress it with the remaining olive oil and lemon.

THE BENEFITS

SALMON
is a great source of the omega 3 fatty acid EPA, which has an anti-inflammatory effect

SPINACH
is a source of iron, which supplies muscles with oxygen to give you energy

PEAS
provide vitamin B1, which helps reduce sugar cravings, and mood-boosting vitamin C

SPICY FISH STEW

Try adding some spice to your seafood for maximum fat-burning effects with this mouth-watering fish stew recipe

INGREDIENTS

Serves 3-4

100g monkfish

4 scallops

100g salmon

A handful of mussels

4 new potatoes, halved

1 red onion, chopped

1 red pepper, chopped

3 cloves of garlic, crushed

1 chilli, diced

1tbsp ginger, chopped

400g canned chopped tomatoes

200ml fish stock

1tbsp saffron

A pinch of cumin

A pinch of paprika

1tbsp olive oil

1tsp lemon juice

1tsp fresh coriander, diced

TO MAKE

▷ Heat the olive oil in a frying pan and cook the potatoes for four minutes on a medium heat.

▷ Add the onion, peppers, garlic, chilli and ginger and sauté for two minutes.

▷ Add the tomatoes and cook on a low heat for five minutes.

▷ Add the fish stock and all the spices and cook for ten minutes.

▷ Add all the fish and cook for eight minutes.

▷ Serve and garnish with the lemon juice and fresh coriander.

THE BENEFITS

SALMON
is a source of the omega 3 fatty acid DHA, which maintains your nervous system

LEMON JUICE
helps to control blood sugar levels and prevent fat storage

TOMATOES
contain lots of immunity-boosting vitamin C.

UNDER
45
MINS

STUFFED WHOLE SALMON

Build a mouth-watering salmon sandwich and enjoy huge muscle gains

INGREDIENTS

Serves 2–3

1 side of salmon

Salt and pepper, to season

500g spinach, blanched

1 tomato, sliced

1 lemon, sliced

TO MAKE

- Preheat the oven to 200°C/gas mark 6.
- Spilt the salmon in half horizontally and lay it skin down on a board.
- Season with salt and black pepper, then position the spinach, tomatoes and lemon evenly across one half of the salmon.
- Lay the second slice on top, skin side up, and tie the slices together with string to keep them in place.
- Roast in the oven for 20 minutes.

THE BENEFITS

SALMON
contains omega 3 fats that help soothe your aching joints after a workout

SPINACH
is rich in bone-strengthening vitamin K

TOMATOES
provide plenty of heart-protecting lycopene

UNDER
15
MINS

TUNA NIÇOISE

This time-saving salad can be prepared in minutes and provides plenty of protein to fuel your workout

INGREDIENTS

Serves 1

100g tuna loin

20g new potatoes

3 quail's eggs

20g green beans

1 gem heart lettuce, shredded

A handful of cherry tomatoes

20g artichokes, halved

20g black olives, pitted

2 anchovies

2 tbsp olive oil

½tsp Dijon mustard

A pinch of chopped parsley

TO MAKE

▷ Slice the new potatoes in half and boil them in a pan of water for ten minutes.

▷ Meanwhile, in two separate pans boil the eggs for four minutes and the green beans for five.

▷ Slice the tuna and pan-fry it lightly for four minutes, turning halfway through.

▷ Mix the lettuce, cherry tomatoes, green beans, artichokes, olives and anchovies in a bowl.

▷ Add the tuna, potatoes and eggs.

▷ Mix together the olive oil and mustard to make a dressing. Drizzle over the salad and dress with the parsley.

THE BENEFITS

TUNA
is high in omega 3 fatty acids, which help to improve joint health

QUAIL'S EGGS
are packed with muscle-building protein

OLIVES
contain heart-healthy polyunsaturated and monounsaturated fats

UNDER
15
MINS

SQUID & CHICKPEA SALAD

It might not sound like an obvious combo, but chorizo and squid form a tasty muscle-building pair in this high-protein salad

INGREDIENTS

Serves 2-3

300g squid, sliced into 1cm rings

400g can chickpeas, rinsed and drained

2 red peppers, sliced

1 bunch of parsley, roughly chopped

1 red chilli, deseeded and chopped

2 garlic cloves, finely chopped

50ml olive oil

100g chorizo, sliced

Juice and zest of half a lemon

TO MAKE

▷ Grill the peppers under a medium heat until they're slightly charred.

▷ Mix the peppers, chickpeas, parsley, chilli and garlic in a large bowl and set to one side.

▷ Heat a large frying pan over a medium heat until it's smoking. Add a splash of olive oil and stir-fry the squid for around 30 seconds.

▷ Scatter the chorizo over the squid and continue to cook for another 30 seconds, then remove from the heat and add to the bowl of peppers.

▷ Season with salt and pepper, dress with lemon juice, zest and remaining oil, and serve.

THE BENEFITS

SQUID is high in protein, energy-giving vitamin B12 and bone-strengthening calcium

CHICKPEAS are a great source of metabolism-boosting manganese and filling fibre

RED PEPPERS are full of vitamins A and C, which help repair the cell damage caused by intense training

PRAWN OMELETTE

This fat-burning, metabolism-boosting omelette can be prepared in minutes, making it an ideal post-gym lunch option

INGREDIENTS

Serves 1

A handful of ready-cooked king prawns

4 eggs

1tbsp diced red onion

1tsp parsley

1tsp diced chillies

1tsp olive oil

TO MAKE

▷ Crack the eggs into a bowl, add the onions, chillies and half the parsley, and whisk until fully mixed.

▷ Heat the olive oil in a frying pan over a medium heat. Add the mixture and stir until it starts to set.

▷ Place the prawns on the top and continue to cook until the omelette is set.

▷ Sprinkle the remaining parsley over the omelette, fold in half and serve.

THE BENEFITS

PRAWNS contain pantothenic acid, which contributes to energy production in the body

RED ONIONS are a source of biotin, which helps control blood sugar levels

CHILLIES contain vitamin B6, which helps you metabolise carbs

FISH & CHIPS

UNDER 45 MINS

Skip the chippy and make this energy-boosting version of the classic British dish at home

INGREDIENTS

Serves 1

1 large cod fillet

2 slices of wholemeal bread, crusts removed

1 egg, lightly whisked

2 sweet potatoes, cut into 2-3cm strips

50g fresh peas

1 knob of butter

½ a lemon

TO MAKE

- Preheat the oven to 200°C/gas mark 6.

- Place the bread in a food processor and blend until it forms crumbs.

- Dip the cod fillet into the whisked egg, then cover with the breadcrumbs. Place on a sheet of greaseproof paper on a tray and bake for 20-25 minutes.

- Coat the sweet potato strips in olive oil, place on a tray and bake for 25-30 minutes.

- Heat the butter in a pan, add the peas and cook for ten minutes. Add a squeeze of lemon and mash until appropriately mushy.

THE BENEFITS

SWEET POTATO
offers slow-release carbs for a sustained energy boost

COD
is a lean source of muscle-building protein

PEAS
are rich in bone-strengthening vitamin K

Pork, **beef** and **lamb** are ideal muscle foods. As well as containing high levels of protein, they're also rich in a variety of extra bulk-boosting nutrients, including magnesium and creatine

OVER **60** MINS

RIB OF BEEF

Roast a perfect rib of muscle-building beef every time with this nutritious recipe

INGREDIENTS

Serves 3-4

1 rib of beef

1tbsp olive oil

Pinch of salt and pepper

TO MAKE

- Preheat the oven to 220°C/gas mark 7.
- Rub the beef with the olive oil, and season with salt and pepper.
- Heat a frying pan until hot and sear the beef on all sides.
- Remove from the pan and place on a rack in a roasting tray. Roast in the oven for 20 minutes.
- Turn the oven down to 160°C/gas mark 2-3 and continue to roast for 20 minutes per 450g for medium or 15 minutes per 450g for rare.
- Remove the beef from the roasting tray, wrap in foil and allow to rest for 30 minutes before serving.

THE BENEFITS

BEEF
contains high levels of muscle-building creatine

OLIVE OIL
is rich in heart-healthy unsaturated fats

PEPPER
is a source of bone-strengthening manganese

UNDER
15
MINS

PEACH BRESAOLA

Prepare a healthy salad in minutes with this simple Italian recipe that's brimming with muscle-building protein

INGREDIENTS

Serves 1

150g of bresaola (cured beef)

1 peach

A handful of rocket salad

2tbsp extra virgin olive oil

1tbsp sherry vinegar

Ground pepper to taste

TO MAKE

▷ Cut the peach into pieces.

▷ Mix the pieces with the bresaola and rocket.

▷ Add the olive oil, sherry vinegar and ground pepper to season.

THE BENEFITS

PEACH
provides vitamins A and C, which help reduce the cell damage caused by intense training

BRESAOLA
is very lean, tender and high in muscle-building protein and creatine.

ROCKET
contains glucosinolates, which have powerful cancer-preventing properties

OVER 60 MINS

BEEF RENDANG CURRY

Swap your takeaway dinner for this fat-burning beef rendang

INGREDIENTS

Serves 3

650g braising steak, cubed

1 onion, roughly chopped

2tbsp chopped fresh ginger

1tbsp chopped garlic

1 lemongrass stalk, outer layer removed and roughly chopped

1tsp turmeric

6 chillies, diced

2tbsp olive oil

6 cardamom pods, crushed

1 cinnamon stick

400ml coconut milk

2tbsp Thai fish sauce

Zest of 1 lime

Coriander sprigs, to garnish

TO MAKE

◗ Put the onion, ginger, garlic, lemongrass, turmeric and chillies into a food processor. Blend to form a smooth purée.

◗ Heat a large pan and add the oil. Fry the paste over a high heat until the paste turns a darker colour.

◗ Add the crushed cardamom pods and the cinnamon and cook for another minute, then add the beef and stir-fry until browned.

◗ Add the coconut milk, fish sauce and lime zest and simmer for 60-90 minutes, stirring occasionally.

◗ Garnish with coriander to taste and serve with rice.

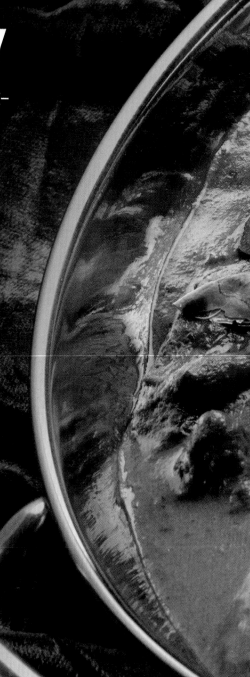

THE BENEFITS

BEEF
contains a range of B vitamins, including energy-boosting B12

ONION
provides quercetin, which has been shown to reduce hay fever symptoms

COCONUT MILK
is high in heart–healthy unsaturated fats

UNDER
15
MINS

FILLET STEAK & VEG

Eat like a primitive man and gorge on steak and vegetables to boost your training results and pack on muscle

INGREDIENTS

Serves 1

1 large fillet steak

A handful of broccoli florets

A handful of cauliflower florets

1 tbsp olive oil

A sprig of thyme

TO MAKE

○ Heat the olive oil in a frying pan

○ Cook the steak for four to 12 minutes according to preference, turning halfway through.

○ Steam the veg for five minutes.

○ Garnish the steak with the thyme and serve.

BROCCOLI
is high in chromium, which the body needs to build muscle, reduce body fat and produce energy

CAULIFLOWER
is rich in folate, which helps produce new muscle cells

OLIVE OIL
contains vitamin E, which helps improve your cholesterol levels

OVER 60 MINS

CHILLI CON CARNE

Build muscle and torch fat with this protein-rich, metabolism-boosting chilli

INGREDIENTS

Serves 2

500g lean beef mince

4 shallots, chopped

2 garlic cloves, chopped

1 red chilli, deseeded and chopped

100ml rapeseed oil

2tsp smoked paprika

3 plum tomatoes, chopped

400g can of chopped tomatoes

150ml beef stock

3tbsp tomato purée

1 bay leaf

400g can of kidney beans, drained

Salt and pepper to taste

1tbsp fresh basil, chopped

Thyme sprigs

2tbsp chives, chopped

200ml Greek yogurt

TO MAKE

▶ Heat half the rapeseed oil in a large saucepan. Add the shallots, garlic and chilli and cook for a few minutes.

▶ At the same time, cook the mince in a separate pan over a moderate heat in the remaining oil. When it's browned, drain in a sieve to remove excess fat.

▶ Add the smoked paprika to the shallot mixture and cook for a further five minutes, then stir in the browned mince.

▶ Add the fresh and tinned tomatoes and leave to reduce on a medium heat for five minutes.

▶ Pour in the beef stock and stir in the tomato purée. Add the bay leaf, then bring the mixture to the boil and leave it to simmer.

▶ Once the sauce is beginning to thicken, which should take 20-30 minutes, add the kidney beans and leave to cook for another five to ten minutes.

▶ Season with salt and pepper and add the basil leaves. Garnish with thyme sprigs.

▶ Mix the chives with the Greek yogurt.

▶ Serve with brown rice (cooked according to packet instructions) and with the chive yogurt on the side.

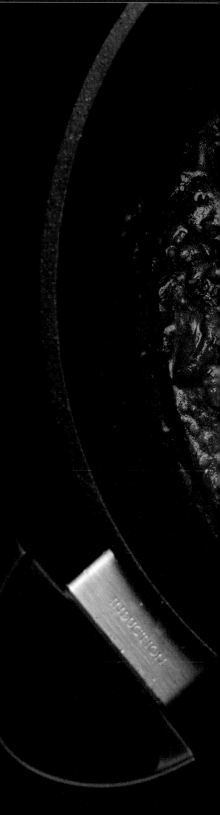

THE BENEFITS

KIDNEY BEANS
are packed with
folate, which helps
to improve mood

SHALLOTS
contain quercetin, which
soothes inflammation
after training

GREEK YOGURT
is high in muscle–
building protein

UNDER
30
MINS

STEAK BURRITO

Wrap your beef and enjoy it with the healthy fats provided by Greek yogurt and guacamole in this classic Mexican meal

INGREDIENTS

Serves 1

1 wholemeal tortilla wrap

50g brown rice

60g black beans

100g steak

1 tomato

A handful of lettuce

1tbsp Greek yogurt

1tsp fresh coriander

1tbsp guacamole

½ a red onion, chopped

TO MAKE

○ Cook the rice according to packet instructions.

○ Meanwhile, chop the lettuce and dice the tomato and coriander, then mix them in a bowl with the black beans.

○ Slice the steak and fry it in olive oil with the onion until well browned.

○ Place the open tortilla on a plate and fill it with the diced steak and vegetable mix.

○ Wrap the tortilla and serve with the guacamole and Greek yogurt.

THE BENEFITS

BEEF
is a source of muscle-building CLA – especially grass-fed beef

BLACK BEANS
are packed with fibre to keep you feeling full for longer

GREEK YOGURT
contains pantothenic acid, which helps convert food into fuel

BURGER & CHIPS

Craving a Big Mac? Have a muscle-building home-made meat feast instead with this easy recipe

INGREDIENTS

Serves 2

400g lean organic beef mince

3 medium sweet potatoes

½tsp mild chilli powder

1tsp paprika

200ml rapeseed oil

1tbsp English mustard

2 wholemeal burger buns

Natural sea salt and ground white pepper

Toppings – your choice of sliced tomatoes, shredded baby gem lettuce

TO MAKE

◗ Preheat the oven to 200°C/gas mark 6. Put a shallow baking tray in the oven to warm.

◗ Wash the sweet potato and cut into even wedges. Place the wedges in a bowl, add the chilli powder and paprika, and mix thoroughly.

◗ Add half the rapeseed oil and mix again.

◗ Place the potato wedges on the warmed baking tray and cook for 20-25 minutes, turning halfway through to ensure they're crisp on both sides.

◗ Meanwhile, place the beef in a bowl, add the mustard, season to taste and mix thoroughly.

◗ Divide the mixture in half and shape into two 2cm-thick patties.

◗ Warm half the remaining rapeseed oil in a frying pan over a medium heat and fry the patties for six minutes on each side for a medium finish, or eight to ten minutes on each side for a well done finish.

◗ Slice the buns in half, brush with the remaining oil and place under a low grill for one minute until warmed.

◗ Place a burger in each bun, finish with any or all of the toppings and serve.

THE BENEFITS

MUSTARD
helps to stimulate circulation to soothe your aching muscles

WHOLEMEAL BUN
has a low GL, ensuring you avoid fat-storing insulin spikes

SWISS CHEESE
is a great source of bone-strengthening calcium

LIVER, BACON & ONIONS

It's not as popular as it used to be, but feast on this suprisingly tasty traditional British dish and you'll reap the muscle-building benefits

INGREDIENTS

Serves 1

200g calf's liver, thinly sliced

3 rashers of streaky bacon

½ an onion, finely sliced

1tbsp olive oil

2tbsp red wine

150ml beef stock

TO MAKE

▷ Fry the onion with half the olive oil in a pan over a low heat.

▷ Add the wine and stock and simmer to reduce until thickened.

▷ Meanwhile, grill the bacon under a medium heat for eight minutes or until crispy, turning halfway through.

▷ Pan-fry the liver in the remaining oil over a high heat for eight minutes, turning halfway through.

THE BENEFITS

ONIONS
are rich in manganese, which helps control blood sugar levels

LIVER
contains a hefty 28g of muscle-building protein per 100g

BACON
provides a hit of energy-boosting B vitamins to fuel your gym sessions

BEEF LASAGNE

Give this rich, cheesy dish a healthy twist with this upgraded recipe

INGREDIENTS

Serves 3-4

500g lean organic beef mince

100ml rapeseed oil

2 red onions, peeled and finely chopped

2 garlic cloves, peeled and crushed

300ml chunky passata

1tsp Worcestershire sauce

A handful of fresh basil, finely chopped

A pinch of sea salt and ground white pepper

3 medium sweet potatoes, peeled and sliced as thinly as possible

500ml low-fat natural yogurt

100g mature cheddar cheese, grated

TO MAKE

- Heat a large thick-bottomed pan over a medium heat.

- Add the oil, onions and garlic and cook for three to four minutes.

- Add the mince, breaking it up with a wooden spoon so it cooks evenly, and cook for five minutes until browned.

- Add the passata and stir. Bring the mixture to the boil and simmer gently for ten minutes. Add the Worcestershire sauce and basil, mixing thoroughly, then season to taste with salt and pepper and remove from the heat.

- Spoon one-third of the mixture into an ovenproof dish, so it covers the bottom. Arrange half the sweet potato slices on top so they completely cover the beef.

- Repeat the process, so you have two layers of beef and two layers of potato, then finish with a final layer of beef.

- Pour the natural yogurt over the top and sprinkle with grated cheese.

- Bake in a preheated oven at 180°C/gas mark 4 for an hour.

- Remove from the oven and allow to stand for ten minutes before serving.

BEEF
provides the omega 3 fat
ALA, which your body
needs for energy

GARLIC
contains sulphur
compounds that reduce
post–exercise muscle
soreness

CHEDDAR
provides a large dose of
muscle–building casein

STEAK BAGUETTE

Don't head to the pub for a steak sandwich – make it at home for more health benefits and less temptation to go afternoon drinking

INGREDIENTS

Serves 2

1 sourdough baguette

2 150g lean organic beef minute steaks

3 medium sweet potatoes

2tbsp wholegrain mustard

150ml rapeseed oil

Salt and pepper to taste

TO MAKE

- Pre-heat an oven to 200°C/ gas mark 6 and place a shallow baking tray inside to heat up.

- Wash the sweet potatoes and cut them into evenly sized finger-length pieces, leaving the skin on.

- Place the sweet potato chips in a bowl, then add three-quarters of the rapeseed oil and mix thoroughly.

- Place the sweet potato chips on the pre-heated tray in the oven and cook for 15–20 minutes, turning them halfway through.

- Rub the remaining rapeseed oil on both sides of the steaks and season them with the salt and pepper.

- Heat a griddle pan to a high heat and place the steaks on it. Cook them for one to two minutes on each side (one minute for a rare finish, two minutes for a well-done finish).

- Slice the baguette in half lengthways. Spread the mustard on one half of and brush a little more rapeseed oil on to the other half.

- Place the steak on the half brushed with the rapeseed oil, then place the mustard half on top to complete the sandwich.

- Remove the sweet potato chips from the oven and serve with the sandwich.

MUSTARD
contains selenium, which has anti-inflammatory properties and can protect against illness

SOURDOUGH BREAD
has a lower GL than white, reducing fat-storing insulin spikes

SWEET POTATO
contains high levels of immunity-boosting vitamins A and C

RACK OF LAMB

Enjoy a full rack of muscle-building lamb with sweet potato mash and vine tomatoes with this easy-to-follow recipe

INGREDIENTS

Serves 2

1 rack of lamb

1 egg

1tsp Dijon mustard

100g breadcrumbs

1 clove of garlic, chopped

2tbsp parsley, chopped

200g sweet potato, mashed

50g butter

8 vine tomatoes

TO MAKE

- Preheat the oven to 200°C/gas mark 6.
- Beat the egg with the mustard, then mix with the breadcrumbs, garlic and chopped parsley.
- Coat the lamb in the egg and herb crust and roast for around 17 minutes until pink inside.
- Meanwhile, peel the sweet potatoes and boil them in water for 15 minutes.
- Mash the potatoes with the butter and season with salt and pepper to taste.
- Place the tomatoes in a roasting dish and cook for 15 minutes.
- Place the lamb on the mash and serve alongside the roasted tomatoes.

THE BENEFITS

LAMB
is packed with the amino acid tryptophan, which helps to regulate appetite

SWEET POTATOES
are high in the antioxidant betacarotene, which helps to lower LDL (bad) cholesterol

TOMATOES
provide plenty of vitamin C, which contributes to your metabolism of amino acids, helping you build muscle

LANCASHIRE HOTPOT

This English classic includes plenty of protein-rich lamb to fuel your workouts and aid new muscle growth

INGREDIENTS

Serves 4-6

900g diced lamb shoulder

2-3tbsp olive oil

3tbsp plain flour

2 carrots, peeled and chopped into 1cm-thick discs

2 onions, peeled and thinly sliced

1 sprig of thyme

1 bay leaf

600ml lamb stock

Salt and pepper to taste

4 large sweet potatoes, peeled and thinly sliced

TO MAKE

▶ Preheat the oven to 170°C/gas mark 3.

▶ Dust the meat lightly with the flour and season it with salt and pepper.

▶ Heat some of the oil in a frying pan over a medium heat and fry the lamb until browned. Remove and set aside.

▶ Add a little more oil and fry the onions and carrots over a low heat until lightly browned.

▶ Place the lamb, carrots and onions in a deep casserole dish and pour in the stock. Add the bay leaf and thyme and stir the mixture thoroughly.

▶ Top with three layers of potato slices, brushing each layer with olive oil and seasoning well.

▶ Bake for 1½ hours or until the meat is tender and the potatoes are crisp around the edges.

▶ Cover the hotpot with foil and leave to stand for ten minutes before serving.

THE BENEFITS

LAMB
is a source of B vitamins and CLA, both of which provide energy

CARROTS
are rich in immune-strengthening betacarotene

SWEET POTATOES
have a lower GL than white potatoes, so they cause less of a blood sugar spike

PORK BELLY

Pork is tasty, comforting and much healthier than you might think

INGREDIENTS

Serves 2

500g organic pork belly

1 onion, chopped

1 clove of garlic

A pinch of thyme

1 star anise

250ml vegetable stock

300g red cabbage, shredded

50ml red wine

2tbsp red wine vinegar

1 apple, diced

1tbsp olive oil

2 handfuls of spinach

TO MAKE

- Place the pork belly in a deep roasting tray with the onion, garlic, thyme and star anise underneath.

- Pour the vegetable stock into the tray, cover with foil and place in an oven, pre-heated to 180°C / gas mark 4, for two hours.

- Once cooked, remove from the oven and allow to rest in the liquid for a further hour.

- Remove the pork from the liquid, place on a clean oven tray and return to the oven to cook at 200°C / gas mark 6 for 20 minutes.

- Place a pan on a medium heat and add the cabbage, red wine, vinegar and apple. Cover and cook for 45 minutes.

- When the cabbage is almost cooked, place another pan over a medium heat, warm the olive oil, add the spinach and cook for two minutes.

- Slice the pork belly and serve on top of the spinach with the cabbage on the side.

PORK
contains muscle-
strengthening magnesium

APPLE
is rich in filling fibre,
which reduces your
desire to snack

RED WINE
contains compounds called
procyanidins, which keep
blood vessels healthy

UNDER
15
MINS

TAPAS PLATTER

Binge on healthy fats and protein, Spanish-style, with a selection of tapas and snacks. Rustic wooden platter optional

INGREDIENTS

Serves 2

1 whole chorizo sausage, sliced

70g sliced serrano ham

A handful of green olives

A handful of black olives

3 small fresh figs

100g manchego cheese

50g anchovies in olive oil

100g roasted peppers

A handful of parsley (optional), to garnish

TO MAKE

◯ Slice the cheese and chorizo.

◯ Chop the parsley.

◯ Arrange all the tapas ingredients on a plate or platter.

OLIVES
are a great source of the monounsaturated fat oleic acid, as well as filling fibre

MANCHEGO CHEESE
is made from sheep's milk, so it's higher in healthy fats than cow's milk cheese

ANCHOVIES
are full of healthy omega 3 fats and muscle-building protein

UNDER
15
MINS

CHORIZO SALAD

Salad may seem a less obvious muscle builder than steak – but this meaty dish is much more than a bunch of limp leaves

INGREDIENTS

Serves 1

75g chorizo, sliced

100g green beans, halved

1 red onion, sliced

1 garlic clove, crushed

1tbsp sherry or red wine vinegar

5 cherry tomatoes, halved

1tbsp olive oil

20g watercress

Wholemeal bread, to serve

TO MAKE

‣ Boil the green beans in a pan for three to four minutes.

‣ In another pan, heat the oil and fry the chorizo for three to four minutes.

‣ Add the onions and garlic to the same pan and fry for a further two minutes.

‣ Add the vinegar and tomatoes to the pan and sizzle for 30 seconds.

‣ Toss the chorizo mixture with the watercress and cooked green beans and serve with the bread.

THE BENEFITS

TOMATOES
contain vitamin C, which helps your body form strong tendons, ligaments and bone

GREEN BEANS
are a source of the mineral silicon, which keeps your bones and connective tissue healthy

GARLIC
has anti-inflammatory, anti-bacterial and anti-viral properties

BANGERS & MASH

Protein-rich sausages alongside healthy fresh veg and good fats make this favourite a muscle-building treat

INGREDIENTS

Serves 2

4 free-range Cumberland sausages

300g new potatoes

50g rapeseed oil

2tbsp natural yogurt

3-4 spring onions, finely sliced

100g baby spinach, washed and drained

Salt and pepper

TO MAKE

- Place the new potatoes in a large pan, cover them with cold water and bring to the boil. Reduce the heat and simmer.

- Meanwhile, place the sausages under a medium grill, turning them occasionally until they're brown on all sides and fully cooked.

- Once the new potatoes are tender, drain them into a colander and leave them to steam for one to two minutes.

- Put the potatoes in a medium-size pan and crush them with a fork.

- Add three-quarters of the oil, the yogurt and the spring onions to the potatoes and mix thoroughly.

- In a separate bowl, add the remaining rapeseed oil to the spinach.

- Spoon a pile of the crushed new potatoes on to a plate and place the baby spinach and sausages on top. Season and serve.

NEW POTATOES
are full of blood pressure–
lowering potassium

SPINACH
is an excellent source
of vitamin K, which
keeps your blood and
bones healthy

SPRING ONIONS
provide chromium, a
mineral that helps maintain
blood sugar levels and
control food cravings

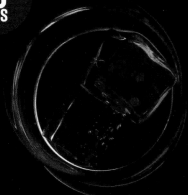

HAM & EGGS

Give ham and eggs a fat-burning upgrade by adding a little-known but very healthy vegetable

INGREDIENTS

Serves 1

3 slices Serrano ham

4tbsp white or white wine vinegar

2 eggs

1tbsp olive oil

50g samphire

TO MAKE

- Bring a pan of water to the boil over a medium heat, then reduce to a simmer.

- Add the vinegar and stir.

- Crack the eggs into the pan and simmer for three minutes.

- Meanwhile, heat the olive oil in a frying pan over a medium heat. Add the samphire and sauté for two minutes.

- Serve the ham and eggs on a bed of samphire.

THE BENEFITS

SAMPHIRE
is a source of vitamins A and C, which work to boost your immune system

EGGS
are full of omega 3 fatty acids, which improve joint health and reduce inflammation

SERRANO HAM
is an excellent source of muscle-building protein with around 30g per 100g

UNDER
30
MINS

ENGLISH BREAKFAST

The classic hangover cure doesn't have to be a trans fat-fest – just choose fresh, high-quality ingredients and be smart about how you cook them

INGREDIENTS

Serves 1

2 free-range pork sausages

2 slices of free-range smoked back bacon

½ a plum tomato

100ml white wine vinegar

1tsp rapeseed oil

2 free-range eggs

1 large mushroom, washed

1 slice of wholemeal bread

TO MAKE

◐ Brush the tomato with rapeseed oil and place under a medium grill with the sausages and bacon. Turn the sausages and bacon occasionally to ensure they cook evenly.

◐ Meanwhile, fill a small saucepan with water until three-quarters full, add the white wine vinegar and bring to the boil.

◐ Crack the eggs into separate cups. Gently pour them one at a time into the pan. Stir the water gently so the eggs spin, and cook for four to five minutes.

◐ Once the eggs are firm, remove with a slotted spoon and place on a piece of kitchen roll to remove moisture.

◐ Place the mushroom under the grill alongside the tomatoes, sausages and bacon for two minutes.

◐ Toast the bread and serve.

THE BENEFITS

RAPESEED OIL
provides omega 3 fats to improve joint health

TOMATOES
contain lycopene, which helps to lower levels of 'bad' LDL cholesterol

MUSHROOMS
contain high levels of filling fibre

BACON & AVOCADO OPEN SANDWICH

Reinvent a popular lunch by swapping the lettuce in your BLT for a serving of avocado, which is packed with healthy fats

INGREDIENTS

Serves 1

2 slices lean, smoked back bacon

1 slice of wholemeal bread

1 ripe avocado, sliced

5 cherry tomatoes, halved

1 tsp unsalted butter

Ground black pepper to taste

TO MAKE

- ◗ Grill the bacon under a medium heat for eight minutes or until crisp, turning halfway through.

- ◗ Meanwhile, toast the bread.

- ◗ Butter the toast, place the bacon on top and layer with the avocado and tomato.

- ◗ Season with pepper to taste and serve.

THE BENEFITS

BACON
contains choline, which improves brain function

TOMATO
contains immunity-boosting vitamin C and heart-healthy vitamin B3

BLACK PEPPER
works as an antioxidant to improve digestion

OVER
60
MINS

PULLED PORK QUESADILLA

This Mexican meal gives a hit of protein in a wholemeal wrap that also provides slow-release carbs to keep your energy levels up

INGREDIENTS

Serves 3–4

2–3 wholemeal tortilla wraps per person

1 medium-sized pork shoulder

3tbsp sea salt

3tbsp muscovado sugar

3tbsp smoked paprika

1tbsp crushed black pepper

100g cheddar or other cheese, grated

Garnish
1 onion, finely sliced

1 small chilli, finely diced

1 small bunch of coriander, chopped

1tsp smoked paprika

Tomato salsa
6 tomatoes, chopped

1 shallot, finely chopped

A dash of Tabasco sauce

A dash of Worcestershire sauce

A pinch of salt

A pinch of sugar

TO MAKE

◗ Preheat the oven to 220°C/gas mark 7.

◗ Place the pork shoulder in a roasting dish. Mix the salt, sugar, paprika and pepper, rub half of it into the pork and place it in the oven for 20 minutes.

◗ Reduce the temperature to 125°C/gas mark 2 and cook for five to six hours, followed by a further 20 minutes at 220°C. Then allow it to rest for 60 minutes.

◗ Pull the meat off the bone using two forks and mix with the remaining seasoning. Mix the garnish ingredients.

◗ Add a generous amount of pulled pork to each tortilla wrap with as much cheese and garnish as required. Roll up, then place under a hot grill until warmed.

◗ Mix the salsa ingredients and serve with the quesadillas alongside a crunchy green salad.

UNDER 30 MINS

SPAGHETTI CARBONARA

Want a creamy but healthy pasta feast? Try this fat-busting variation

INGREDIENTS

Serves 2

120g smoked pancetta, sliced

220g wholemeal spaghetti

4 free-range egg yolks

6tbsp low-fat natural yogurt

6tbsp Lancashire cheese, grated

1tbsp rapeseed oil

White pepper, to taste

TO MAKE

▷ Add the rapeseed oil to a pan of boiling water and cook the spaghetti according to its packet instructions.

▷ While the spaghetti is cooking, fry the pancetta – without any oil – until it's crisp and golden. Place the pancetta on some kitchen paper to soak up any excess grease and set it to one side.

▷ Whisk the egg yolks and natural yogurt in a bowl, season generously with the white pepper and then add 4tbsp of the grated cheese.

▷ When it's ready, drain the spaghetti quickly into a colander, leaving a little of the moisture still clinging to it. Quickly return it to the saucepan and add the pancetta and the egg and yogurt mixture.

▷ Stir thoroughly until all the spaghetti is covered.

▷ Place the pasta in a bowl or on a plate and sprinkle the remaining grated cheese over it.

EGGS
offer plenty of energy–
boosting vitamin B2

WHOLEMEAL SPAGHETTI
contains manganese,
which protects against
the cell damage caused
by free radicals

NATURAL YOGURT
is a source of stress–
reducing vitamin B12

UNDER
15
MINS

PEA & HAM SOUP

Fuel your fat loss with this hearty soup, which is high in protein and low in carbs and sugar, so it won't give you fat-storing blood sugar spikes.

INGREDIENTS

Serves 2

100g shredded ham hock

2tbsp rapeseed oil

1 medium-sized onion, chopped

1 medium-sized sweet potato, cut into small cubes

300g frozen garden peas

300ml vegetable stock

100ml semi-skimmed milk

A small handful of fresh mint leaves

1tsp chopped chives

Salt and pepper to taste

TO MAKE

▷ Heat the oil in a pan over a medium heat.

▷ Add the onion and sweet potato, season with the salt and pepper and fry for three minutes, stirring continuously.

▷ Add the peas and stock, bring to the boil and simmer for four minutes.

▷ Add the milk, bring back to the boil and then take off the heat.

▷ Blend the soup in a food processor until smooth.

▷ Serve it in a bowl and garnish it with the ham, chives and mint leaves.

THE BENEFITS

SWEET POTATO
is the best dietary source of vitamin A, which is crucial to cell growth and fights infection

PEAS
are high in bone-strengthening vitamin K

HAM
is packed with metabolism-boosting thiamin

EGGS & DAIRY

You don't have to eat something that had a face to build muscle. These vegetarian-friendly recipes bring you protein in the form of **milk**, **cheese** and **eggs**

UNDER
15
MINS

FRENCH TOAST

Here's how to turn eggs and bread into a supercharged, fat-burning meal to kick-start your morning

INGREDIENTS

Serves 1

2 eggs

2 tbsp milk

A pinch of salt

1 tbsp sugar

A pinch of cinnamon

2 slices of sourdough bread

2 tbsp butter

1 tbsp Greek yogurt

2 tsp honey

A handful of mixed berries

TO MAKE

◇ Whisk together the eggs, milk, salt, sugar and cinnamon in a bowl.

◇ Submerge the bread in the mixture, ensuring each slice is fully covered.

◇ Melt the butter in a frying pan and fry each slice for two minutes on each side.

◇ Serve with the yogurt, berries and honey.

THE BENEFITS

GREEK YOGURT
has 8g of protein per 100g, alongside a hit of energising vitamin B12

EGGS
contain iron and vitamin A, both of which play a vital role in immune system health

BERRIES
are high in fibre for a healthy gut and packed with cell-protecting antioxidants

UNDER 15 MINS

GOAT'S CHEESE SALAD

This light and flavoursome salad still packs in serious protein, thanks to goat's cheese and pine nuts

INGREDIENTS

Serves 1

30g goat's cheese, cubed

3 beetroots, sliced

A handful of spinach

1tbsp pine nuts

1tbsp olive oil

½tbsp balsamic vinegar

TO MAKE

▷ Wash the spinach and slice the beetroot.

▷ Mix the spinach, beetroot, goat's cheese and pine nuts.

▷ Dress with the olive oil and balsamic vinegar and serve.

THE BENEFITS

GOAT'S CHEESE
is packed with protein and low in salt

BEETROOT
is an excellent source of the energy-boosting vitamin folate

SPINACH
contains a huge range of vitamins, minerals and fibre

UNDER
15
MINS

BLUEBERRY PECAN PORRIDGE

Start your day right with this quick and tasty breakfast recipe

INGREDIENTS

Serves 1

200ml milk

50g porridge oats

1tbsp manuka honey

2tbsp pecan nuts, halved

A handful of blueberries

TO MAKE

▷ Put the milk and oats in a pan.

▷ Cook over a medium heat for eight minutes, stirring occasionally.

▷ Top with the remaining ingredients and serve immediately.

THE BENEFITS

MILK
contains both slow- and fast-relase protein and calcium, which helps your body to metabolise fat

MANUKA HONEY
contains methylglyoxal, an antibacterial agent that helps the body to fight infection

PECAN NUTS
are high in muscle-building protein and heart-healthy unsaturated fats

BROCCOLI & STILTON SOUP

Get loads of goodness in one simple-to-prepare dish with this tasty soup

INGREDIENTS

Serves 1

1tbsp stilton, crumbled

250g broccoli, cut into florets

1tbsp olive oil

½ an onion, diced

1 garlic clove, crushed

A handful of spinach

150ml vegetable stock

1tbsp toasted almonds

Salt and pepper

TO MAKE

▷ Heat the oil in a pan over a medium heat. Add the onion and garlic and cook until softened.

▷ Add the broccoli, spinach and stock and bring to the boil.

▷ Remove the mixture from the pan and blend until smooth.

▷ Serve with the crumbled stilton and toasted almonds on top.

THE BENEFITS

BROCCOLI
is high in chromium, which the body needs to build muscle, reduce body fat and produce energy.

GARLIC
can help to lower cholesterol and protect blood vessels from oxidative stress.

OLIVE OIL
provides unsaturated fats, which help improve your HDL and LDL cholesterol levels

UNDER
15
MINS

CAPRESE SALAD

Enjoy the cuisine of the sun-kissed Italian south and build muscle at the same time with a mozzarella and tomato feast

INGREDIENTS

Serves 1

1 pack of buffalo mozzarella, torn into chunks

2 large vine tomatoes, sliced

8 cherry tomatoes, halved

8 small basil leaves

2 tbsp extra virgin olive oil

Salt and pepper to taste

TO MAKE

- Arrange the slices of tomato on a large plate in a circle, overlapping slightly.
- Top with the halved cherry tomatoes and the torn mozzarella.
- Sprinkle the basil leaves on top and drizzle the olive oil over the plate.
- Season with salt and pepper and serve.

THE BENEFITS

TOMATOES provide plenty of free radical-fighting lycopene

BASIL contains high levels of bone-strengthening vitamin K

OLIVE OIL is rich in oleic acid, which helps to lower blood pressure

GOAT'S CHEESE-STUFFED BUTTERNUT SQUASH

Enjoy a hearty, warming dish of sweet roasted veg that also builds muscle

INGREDIENTS

Serves 2

100g goat's cheese

1 butternut squash, halved

A pinch of chilli flakes

1tsp thyme

1 garlic clove, crushed

2tsp olive oil

1 courgette, chopped

1 red pepper, chopped

50g pine nuts

100g cherry tomatoes, halved

1tbsp chopped parsley

1tbsp grated parmesan

TO MAKE

▷ Heat the oven to 180°C/gas mark 4. Criss-cross the flesh of each squash half with a sharp knife.

▷ Mix the chilli, thyme, garlic and olive oil and brush the flesh with the mixture.

▷ Roast the squash in a roasting tin for 40 minutes.

▷ In a separate roasting tin, roast the pepper and courgette for 25 minutes.

▷ Remove the squash from the oven and stuff with the roasted pepper and courgette, goat's cheese, pine nuts and tomatoes, then roast for further ten minutes.

▷ Sprinkle grated parmesan and chopped fresh parsley over the top, then serve.

THE BENEFITS

GOAT'S CHEESE
is high in vitamins
D and K for strong bones

COURGETTE
is a source of manganese,
which helps the body
produce testosterone.

PINE NUTS
are full of protein,
vitamin A and healthy
monounsaturated fats

BERRY BREAKFAST SUNDAE

Ditch the breakfast cereal and raise a glass with this nutritious berry and yogurt treat, topped with almonds and honey

INGREDIENTS

Serves 1

200g Greek yogurt

100g strawberries

100g raspberries

100g blueberries

30g almonds

1tbsp honey

TO MAKE

▷ Slice the strawberries and mix with the blueberries and raspberries.

▷ Put half the fruit mixture into a sundae glass, then add half the yoghurt.

▷ Add the remaining fruit and the remaining yoghurt.

▷ Top the whole thing with almonds and honey.

THE BENEFITS

BERRIES
are high in vitamins A, C and D, and contain phytochemicals that help protect against cancer

GREEK YOGURT
contains muscle-building protein as well as B vitamins that help convert food into fuel

ALMONDS
are high in protein and also contain selenium, which helps protect against heart disease

EGGS FLORENTINE

For a simple and delicious twist on eggs at breakfast, try this Italian-inspired recipe, with spinach and a wholemeal muffin

INGREDIENTS

Serves 1

1 medium egg

1 wholemeal muffin

2tbsp hollandaise sauce (shop bought is fine)

A handful of spinach

1tbsp olive oil

A pinch of salt

4tbsp white wine vinegar

A pinch of cayenne pepper

1tsp fresh chives, diced

TO MAKE

- Bring a pan of water to the boil and add the salt and white wine vinegar.
- Crack the egg into the pan and let it simmer for three minutes.
- While the egg is cooking, slice and lightly toast the muffin, heat the hollandaise sauce in a pan over a low heat until warmed through and cook the spinach in a pan with the olive oil for two minutes on a low heat.
- Remove the egg with a slotted spoon and serve with the muffin, sauce and spinach.
- Garnish with the chives and pepper.

THE BENEFITS

EGGS
contain all the crucial amino acids your muscles need to grow

SPINACH
contains zinc, which helps you produce the muscle-building hormone testosterone

OLIVE OIL
is a great source of heart-healthy monounsaturated and polyunsaturated fats

UNDER
15
MINS

TURKISH EGGS

Spice up your breakfast and build muscle with this high-protein Turkish recipe that's also rich in healthy fats

INGREDIENTS

Serves 1

2 eggs

1½ cloves of garlic, crushed

100g Greek yogurt

20ml extra virgin olive oil

10g unsalted butter

½ tsp dried chilli flakes

1 stalk of fresh flat-leaf parsley, chopped

25ml white wine vinegar

TO MAKE

▷ Mix the garlic with the yogurt and half the olive oil. Whisk for ten seconds and put to one side.

▷ Melt the butter in a small pan until it is a nutty brown colour. Remove from the heat, add the chilli and stir, allowing it to sizzle.

▷ Add the remaining oil and the parsley, then set aside.

▷ Add the vinegar to a deep pan of simmering water and poach the eggs.

▷ Serve the eggs in a bowl on top of the yogurt mixture and pour the olive oil/butter mixture over the top.

EGGS
are a source of essential amino acids and testosterone-boosting zinc

GREEK YOGURT
is low-GL, so it helps to keep blood sugar levels steady and prevent energy crashes.

CHILLI FLAKES
are a source of capsaicin, which has pain-killing and heart-protecting properties

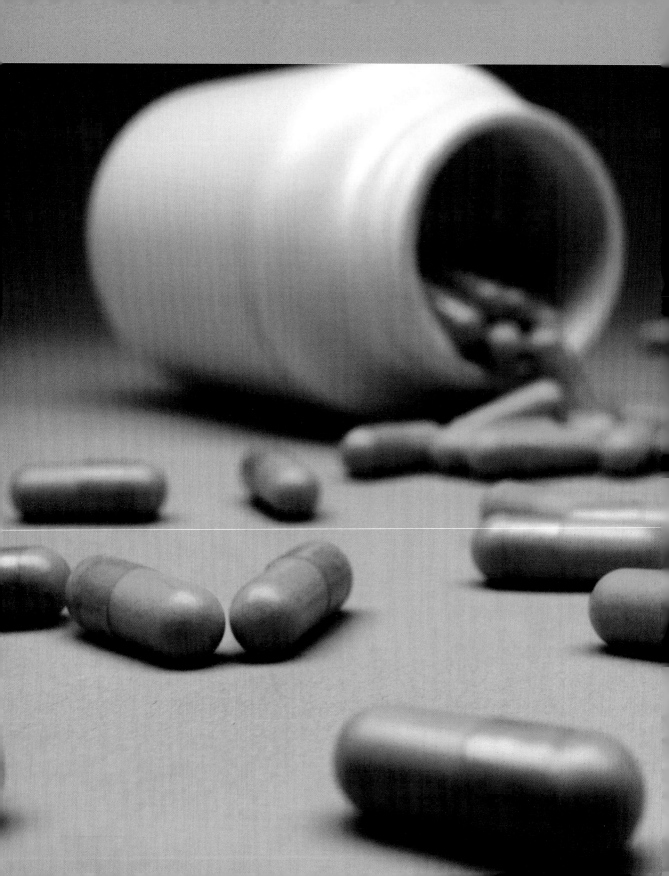

A LITTLE HELP?

Nutritional supplements can optimise the fitness-boosting effect of your diet

The meals in this book contain all the nutrients you need to build an impressive physique. But even if your diet's great, you can always use a little more help to pack on muscle mass, burn fat or protect your body from the riggers of strenuous exercise. That's where supplements come in.

Trouble is, they can be a bit confusing, especially since every supplier claims that its brand is the best. But you don't need a degree in chemistry to understand what you're putting into your body. You just need this straightforward guide, which details what you need and when you need it.

So read on and find out how pills and powders can provide all the nutritional back-up you need – and give yourself every chance of sending your training gains through the roof.

WHEY PROTEIN

Whey protein is made from cow's milk and comes in different forms such as isolate, concentrate and hydrolysate. The great thing about whey is that it's rapidly and easily absorbed, making it ideal to take during the critical post-workout window when your body is primed for building muscle. Whey protein can also lower hunger levels due to its influence on the hormone ghrelin, which can be very useful when you're trying to lose weight. Take whey protein within ten minutes of completing your workout to take advantage of the temporary rise in protein synthesis that will boost recovery. If you're vegan or intolerant to dairy products, there are alternative non-dairy and vegan options available. Just make sure you avoid high-carb versions because they could mess up your fat loss.
How much? 25g blended with 200ml water
When? Immediately after training

MULTIVITAMINS

A high-quality multivitamin can go a long way, and if you have to choose one supplement, it would make sense to go for this one as it'll ensure you're getting the widest variety of vitamins and minerals possible.

Of course, a multivitamin won't supply the same amount of individual minerals – such as magnesium and zinc (see p160) – as products dedicated to these nutrients, but it's still helpful as far as overall health and wellbeing go if your budget is tight.

How much? Two capsules a day
When? One with breakfast, one with lunch

OMEGA 3 FATTY ACIDS

The benefits of omega 3s are numerous. They have a profound impact on your overall wellbeing by improving cardiovascular health, speeding up the removal of harmful substances from your body and providing potent anti-inflammatory reactions.

Omega 3s are also anabolic (muscle-building), partly due to their influence on the mTOR pathway that produces muscle growth, but also because they improve insulin sensitivity, which furthers anabolic potential and your ability to burn fat.

How much? 10g a day
When? With breakfast

BCAAs

Branched-chain amino acids (BCAAs) are made up of three essential amino acids: leucine, isoleucine and valine. These are used before and after training to help the body repair and grow new muscle tissue. Leucine activates the complex compound mTOR, which is responsible for elevating muscle protein synthesis and consequently muscle growth. Leucine also increases insulin production, which will help to shuttle those all-important muscle-building proteins to your cells post-workout.

Valine is useful during workouts because it combats another amino acid called tryptophan, which is associated with muscle fatigue. It reduces the uptake of tryptophan across the blood-brain barrier, which helps keep you lifting harder and longer. Look for a BCAA product with a high leucine content, ideally on a 4-1-1 or at least 2-1-1 ratio to maximise its benefits.

How much? 10,000mg a day
When? Half directly before and half directly after training

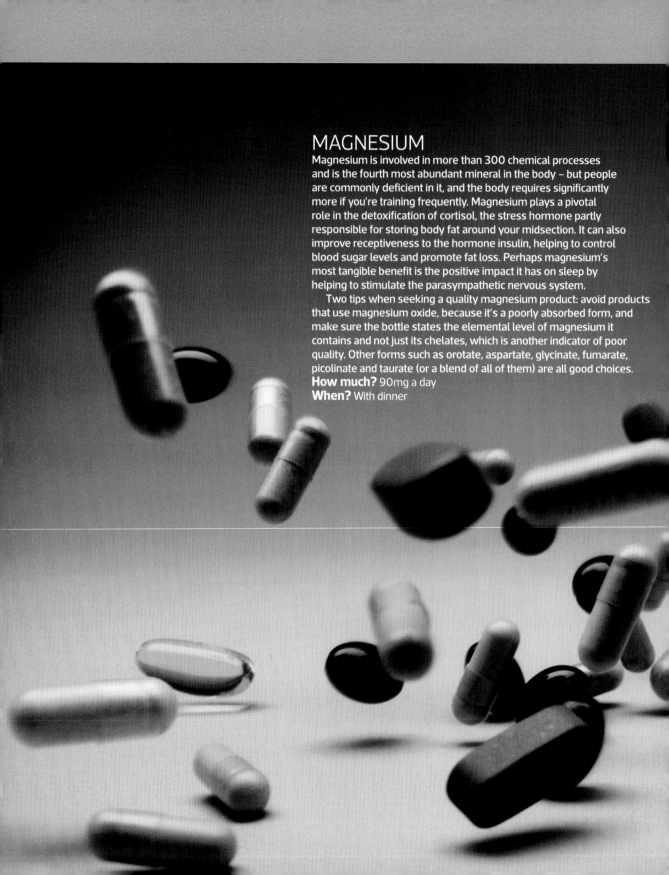

MAGNESIUM

Magnesium is involved in more than 300 chemical processes and is the fourth most abundant mineral in the body – but people are commonly deficient in it, and the body requires significantly more if you're training frequently. Magnesium plays a pivotal role in the detoxification of cortisol, the stress hormone partly responsible for storing body fat around your midsection. It can also improve receptiveness to the hormone insulin, helping to control blood sugar levels and promote fat loss. Perhaps magnesium's most tangible benefit is the positive impact it has on sleep by helping to stimulate the parasympathetic nervous system.

Two tips when seeking a quality magnesium product: avoid products that use magnesium oxide, because it's a poorly absorbed form, and make sure the bottle states the elemental level of magnesium it contains and not just its chelates, which is another indicator of poor quality. Other forms such as orotate, aspartate, glycinate, fumarate, picolinate and taurate (or a blend of all of them) are all good choices.

How much? 90mg a day
When? With dinner

ZINC

Much like magnesium, zinc plays a variety of roles in improving health and performance. It's found in every tissue in the body and is one of the most common of all mineral deficiencies, especially in men. Having correct zinc levels allows for a bigger release of the three most anabolic hormones: testosterone, growth hormone and insulin-like growth factor 1 (IGF-1). If you want to capitalise on your hard work in the gym, you need an abundance of these in your system.

It also has many broader health benefits, such as reducing the risk of prostate cancer, increasing fertility and libido and improving cardiovascular health. As with magnesium, you should try to avoid zinc oxide products and make sure the label clearly states the elemental levels per serving.

How much? 50mg a day
When? With breakfast

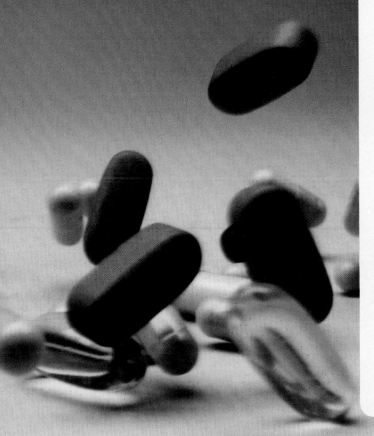

THE BEST OF THE REST

CREATINE
is metabolised by the body into adenosine triphosphate (ATP), which is used during muscle contraction. It's important to have adequate amounts in your body in order to carry out intense weight training sessions. Take 5g before your workout and 5g with a post-workout shake. Be sure to drink plenty of water with it to avoid dehydration.

VITAMIN D
is produced by the body when the skin comes into contact with sunlight. Deficiency, which is associated with severe fatigue and bone weakness, is common in the UK because of our lack of sunshine. Take at least 1,000mg a day.

BETA-ALANINE
is a type of amino acid that works as a lactate buffer during intense training sessions to help you force out extra reps. Take 1,500mg a day.

L-CARNITINE
encourages the body to use fat as a fuel source, spares muscle glycogen and improves the anabolic hormone response to training. Take 2g a day.

SUPER GREENS
provide a big dose of nutrients that would be difficult to achieve from vegetables alone, while keeping you anabolic, thanks to its anti-inflammatory properties and alkalising effects. Take 30g a day.

THYROID SUPPORT
contains l-tyrosine and iodine and will help increase levels of thyroid hormones, a deficit of which can lead to a sluggish metabolism and fat storage. Take 500mg a day.

GLUTAMINE
is the most abundant amino acid in the body but you can add a supplement to your post-workout shake to help with glycogen replenishment. Take 10g a day.

TRY 5 ISSUES FOR JUST £5

and be at the top of your game all year round

Claim 5 issues of Men's Fitness for £5

Visit **dennismags.co.uk/mensfitness**

Or call **0844 844 0081**

Quoting offer code **G1402BMB** for print + digital or **G1402PMB** for print only